G000066200

LEARN H(

PLAY GOLF

FRANK J. PETER

2nd Revised Edition

Copyright © 2007 - 2020 Frank J Peter

ISBN: 9781699064603
Independently published

TERMS OF USE

Limit of Liability and Disclaimer of Warranty

The publisher has used its best efforts in preparing this book, and the information provided herein is provided "as is." Author and publisher make no representation or warranties with respect to the accuracy or completeness of the contents of this book and specifically disclaims any implied warranties of merchantability or fitness for any particular purpose and shall in no event be liable for any loss of profit or any other commercial damage, including but not limited to special, incidental, consequential, or other damages.

Trademarks

This book identifies product names and services known to be trademarks, registered trademarks, or service marks of their respective holders. They are used throughout this book in an editorial fashion only. Use of a term in this book should not be regarded as affecting the validity of any trademark, registered trademark, or service mark. Author and publisher are not associated with any product or vendor mentioned in this book.

Copyright Notice

TABLE OF CONTENTS

WHY PLAY GOLF?

Young sports fans may think of golf as a boring game only played by older individuals. Seniors may worry about keeping up with the youngsters or being too old to learn how to play. Well, I have good news for both types of people...

Golf offers mental and physical challenges for all ages. The goal of the game is simple – to hit a small ball into distant holes. However, the strategy involved is not so simple. Unlike many other sports, there are different ways to achieve this goal.

Planning an attack on a certain hole requires mental strategy. So does finding a way out of trouble when your ball doesn't cooperate. You need to know exactly where and when to attack.

Fast moving games like football or hockey offer you little time to think. Not so in golf. Golfers have plenty of time to plan their most effective method of attack. Ironically, you'll find a lot of golfers not thinking at all. They don't realize the importance of strategy when learning to master this game.

All golf courses contain a series of holes that you try to reach in the least amount of swings. However, the physical layout can vary greatly. Some have sand or water traps and different levels of difficulty depending on the hole placement.

In addition to the actual course, other variables can affect your performance. These include weather changes, wind and moisture, as well as your own temperament. You may find yourself playing very well one day, just to have it come crashing down during your next game. Golf is certainly not predictable!

Another advantage is that golf is a very low-risk game. But don't let this fool you into thinking it's a boring sport. Young golfers quickly realize that golf can be just as challengingly as any other sport, if not more so!

Golf does require some level of endurance. Unless you rent a golf cart, you'll have to walk a lot. A certain amount of strength is also required for your swing. Good eyesight will help you read the subtle contours of the green. The ability to remain calm under pressure will help as you attempt to sink that three-foot putt.

Here are some of the many reasons to learn this interesting game:

- ✓ Anyone can play golf because of the low risk of injury and accidents. Men and women of all ages and physical abilities can enjoy the game.
- ✓ The vast open spaces of a golf course provide plenty of fresh air and the lush scenery helps reduce tension and stress.
- ✓ Golf is a great meeting place for business. In fact, more contracts are said to be signed on the golf course than in the office!
- ✓ Golf offers a great opportunity for social contacts. Many new friends are met during a game of golf.
- ✓ Golf offers both mental and physical challenges, from the swift swing of a long tee-off to the gentle touch of a two-foot putt. Golfers need to strategize and problem solve when dealing with a course's many hazards.
- ✓ Golf offers plenty of walking. The sport offers a terrific form of exercise.
- ✓ Golf doesn't require a partner. You can set your own personal goals.
- ✓ Professional golfers can earn a lot of money.
- ✓ Last but not least, playing golf is fun!

Like any new venture, you should start by testing the waters. You may have friends who already play golf. In fact, some of them may have asked you to join them for a game which you always politely decline. Now is the time to reach for the phone and call one of those friends! If you have a long list, contact an individual who has a lot of free time and lives nearby.

Don't worry if none of your friends play golf. I'm sure at least one of them will know someone who plays the game. Ask your friend to introduce you to this person. If this individual is also a beginner, so much the better. You and your potential golfing buddy can learn together!

GOLF BASICS

The simple object of this game is to hit a small spherical object called a golf ball into a hole using a piece of equipment called a golf club.

Technically, all you need is one golf club and one golf ball. You can perform this task with one stroke or one hundred strokes. Of course, your goal is to sink the ball with as few strokes as possible. That is where the difficulty lies.

Now you need to find a place where you can sink your ball. These are called golf courses.

ELEMENTS OF THE GOLF COURSE

Tee Sign/Layout

As you walk to the first hole, you will notice a tee sign, a board telling you all about the current hole.

The picture on the right shows a tee sign. It usually includes a diagram of the shape of fairway leading to the green with hazards marked along the way.

The first row always indicates the number of the hole. In this case, the layout shows HOLE 1.

The second row, 'PAR 4', tells you that a skilled golfer should require 4 strokes to successfully sink his ball into this hole. Pars are determined by the distance from the tee box to the actual hole. Generally, a Par 3 hole is less than 250 yards, a Par 4 averages between 251 and 475 yards and a Par 5 is any greater distance.

The third row, 'INDEX 11', shows you the relatively difficulty of the hole. Index 1 is the most difficult hole and Index 18 is the easiest. This hole is ranked 11th which is quite an easy hole.

Following the Index are three colored circles with corresponding numbers. The numbers indicate the distance from each of the colored tee boxes. Some courses have four tee boxes and may show distances in meters.

Tee Box

The tee box is where you start off at each hole. It's not actually a box, but a virtual rectangle formed by two colored markers. The color corresponds to that on the layout board, generally 'blue' for low handicappers, 'white' or 'yellow' for average and high handicappers and 'red' for ladies.

If you draw a straight line connecting both markers, you have the front line of the tee box. The back line is at a distance of two club-lengths. You can place your ball anywhere between these two lines and in between the two markers. This is the only place where you are allowed to "tee up" your ball before taking a swing.

According to golf rules, only the ball can be placed inside the tee box. You may stand outside of the tee box to hit the ball.

Fairway

When hitting your ball, you want it to stop on the fairway. This is an area of closely mowed grass along the way from the tee box to the green. A fairway is like a passageway to the green, clearly distinguishable from the rough and from hazards (see below). It isn't always continuous and it varies in width and direction. A bend of the fairway to the right or left is called a 'dog leg'.

Rough

As we all know, where you want to hit the ball may not be where it actually lands. At some point in the game, you may find your ball flying into the long grass or trees. The collective name for these undesirable areas is the rough. You will see rough on either side of the fairway. It's harder to hit the ball out of a rough than from the fairway. If the rough is really bad, hit the ball on to the nearest fairway.

Most rough will include trees. These areas are also called jungles. Surprisingly, some jungles are preferable to the rough before them. That's because the trees discourage long grass from growing underneath. You will often see bare patches of ground that offer a better shot than the thick grass beyond.

Hazards

Hazards are traps purposely designed to increase the difficulty of the course. The number of hazards corresponds to the difficulty and challenge of a particular course. There are two kinds of hazards.

Water Hazard

As the name implies, a water hazard is one that contains water. They can be man-made or natural ponds filled with water. Natural hazards include rivers, lakes, creeks or the sea.

Normal Water Hazard

A Normal water hazard lies across the fairway and is defined by yellow stakes.

Lateral Water Hazard

Golf courses can also contain a lateral water hazard. This stretch of water lies alongside the fairway and is marked by red stakes.

Bunkers

Bunkers or sand traps are pits filled with sand. You'll find fairway bunkers placed in strategic positions along the fairway to trap your ball. If you're unfortunate enough to hit your ball into one, you can walk in and hit your ball out without paying a penalty. However, you're not allowed to touch the sand with your club before your actual stroke.

Bunkers that guard the green are called greenside bunkers and courses usually contain more than one.

Surprisingly, some golfers prefer to play from the bunker than from the rough surrounding the green. Experienced golfers can control bunker shots.

Green

No golf course is complete without the green. This refers to the lovely piece of ground where you hope to find your ball after a swing.

The grass in a green differs from that in the fairway or rough. It can be either

Bermuda grass or Bent grass. The type of grass will influence the speed of the ball.

No two greens are alike. Some greens are quite flat and easy to putt, whereas others have slopes to test your skills. In this territory, you are playing a different game entirely. No more of those hefty swings and chops. This area requires finesse and will test your nerves. This is the game within a game that will determine the final outcome.

The Flagstick

It is often difficult to see the hole because of the long distance. This is where the flagstick comes into play. Basically, it's a long pole with a flag or plastic placard on top. The color of the flag indicates where the hole is relative to the green. Red is used for holes located in the front part of the green. White is used for holes located in the middle and blue is used for holes at the back end of the green. The difference between red and blue holes may require the use of another club. Some clubs may use a different set of colors.

Hole

There is nothing sweeter than hearing the sound of your ball dropping into the hole. The hole, or cup, has a diameter of four and a quarter inches. It must be at least four inches deep.

You have to sink the ball into the hole in order to complete your play. Otherwise, you will be penalized.

A BRIEF HISTORY OF GOLF

A bored shepherd saw a small pebble near a rabbit hole and tried to knock it in with his crook. His companion became interested and tried another pebble with his crook. Bored with the rabbit hole, they looked for another and another.

The game of golf was born! Well, maybe…

The origin of golf differs throughout the world. Most countries associate the sport with sticks and balls with no mention of a rabbit hole. Regardless of the claims, the Scots indisputably popularized the game.

In 1754, the St Andrews Society of Golfers was formed and golf was recognized as a sport. In 1764, an 18-hole course was constructed and St Andrews became the standard for all others to emulate. In 1854, the famous clubhouse was erected. Thereafter, the Royal and Ancient Golf Club of St Andrews (R&A) became the flag-bearer of the game as a sport.

By this time, some clubheads were bulbous and made of wood, whereas others were constructed of hand-forged iron. Shafts were usually made of ash or hazel. Balls consisted of compressed feathers wrapped with leather. Called the "featherie", this ball was laboriously made by hand. Due to the high cost of this handcrafted equipment, the game wasn't available to ordinary citizens.

In 1820, the first golf club outside Britain called the Bangalore appeared in India. Clubs in other countries such as Ireland, France, Australia, Canada, South Africa, USA and Hong Kong began to make an appearance in the 19th century. The St Andrews of New York was the club that started the craze in the US.

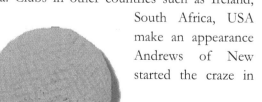

The "guttie", a more durable ball made of gutta-percha, eventually replaced the expensive '"featherie" ball. Metal clubheads and shafts began to appear in the mid 19th century. Mass production made the game affordable to the average person and contributed to the phenomenal growth of the sport.

In the olden days, a golf club was made entirely of wood and resembled the shape of a hockey stick. Clubheads were originally made from holly, beech and pear. Shafts were constructed of ash or hazel. The head was secured to the shaft using a splint wound with leather straps. Clubs were costly because of the painstaking labor involved. Moreover, these clubs weren't durable; golfers would often break 1 or 2 clubs during a single round. Thus, the game wasn't affordable for common folks.

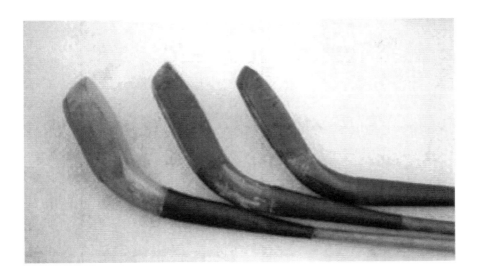

In 1848, Rev. Adam Paterson invented the "Guttie" – a hard rubber gutta-percha golf ball. This ball proved too much for the longnoses. To cope with the higher stress of this ball, manufacturers used additional wood to reinforce the clubhead. These clubs or 'bulgers' had bulbous heads and resembled modern day woods.

The durable Guttie gave rise to the creation of clubs with iron heads. These clubs were aptly called irons. Although they could perform high rising shots, they couldn't out-distance shots by wooden clubheads. These longer-hitting 'woods' retained their wooden clubheads with persimmon as the choice material.

In the 1920s, the first steel-shafted clubs began to appear in the US. In 1931, Billy Burke was the first person to win the US Open with steel shaft clubs. At this time, the sand wedge was being developed.

In 1939, the R&A imposed a limit of 14 clubs that a golfer could use in tournaments. Clubs were also assigned numbers instead of names. Woods were numbered one through five, and irons two through nine. The putter retained its name instead of being assigned a number.

In 1963, mass production of clubheads was made possible by casting. This lowered the price of clubs. However, professionals still preferred hand-forged clubs because of their superior 'feel' and control.

In 1973, the graphite shaft was introduced. Graphite was lighter, stronger and more rigid than steel. Modern graphite shafts included a matrix or other materials for better performance. Currently, many golfers use steel shafts because they're cheaper. Most professionals use steel shafts because they are easier to control.

The most successful club in history is the Big Bertha manufactured by Callaway in 1991. This club has an oversized persimmon wooden clubhead. Taylor-Made became the first company to manufacture metal woods. The current trend is woods with titanium heads that are fitted with graphite shafts.

Changes

The United States Golf Association (USGA) was formed in 1894. The organization established rules and managed the handicap system to enable fair competition among golfers of different standards. In 1900, golf was included into the Olympics. By this time, more than 1000 clubs existed in the USA.

The 20th century saw many technological changes. The first change involved the ball. The Haskell ball had a single rubber core and could travel a longer distance. Grooved-faced irons were introduced. In 1905, William Taylor invented a ball with a dimpled surface. Steel-shafted clubs were produced in 1910. Golfers found they could hit further and more accurately with relatively cheaper equipment.

In 1916, the Professional Golfers Association (PGA) was formed. However, game rules amongst the various countries weren't standardized. In 1921, the R&A imposed a limit on a golf ball's size and weight. Today, the game is governed jointly by the R&A and the USGA. These two bodies meet every four years to update the rules and regulations.

GETTING STARTED

Introduction to Golf Clubs for Beginners

(Note: A whole section on Equipment will deal with the details later in this book, while the following serves as a primer.)

Now that you're involved in the game, you need some of your own equipment. You shouldn't continue to rely on borrowing your friend's equipment.

The rule of golf forbids you to borrow a club from another golfer during a round. You can borrow a set of clubs before starting the round. However, to fully enjoy the game, you need to play with your own set of clubs.

You may be tempted to go out and buy a brand new set of the latest clubs. Don't. Not only will you waste your hard-earned money, you may become the laughing stock of the course with your 100 dollar club and 2 dollar shot!

Basically, there are three types of clubs: the wood, the irons and the putter.

As a beginner, you should start off with a total of 13 clubs. They should include three woods (driver, 3-wood & 5-wood), nine irons (3-9, pitching wedge & sand wedge) and a putter.

As you learn more about different clubs, you'll probably hear the word 'loft'. This refers to the angle made by the clubface when vertical - a perpendicular line drawn from the ground. The measurement is given in degrees. The higher the number, the greater the loft. The greater the loft, the higher the ball will travel.

It's important to know the function of each club and how far it can hit.

Driver

This is the biggest weapon in a golfer's arsenal. The driver is the longest club, apart from some fancy putters, and offers the greatest distance. Its loft is eleven degrees or less, enabling it to hit a low-flying ball. Unfortunately, the driver is also the biggest nemesis. Its length often makes it harder to control. As a beginner, you should start off with a 3-wood or lesser club.

Woods

These are the long range clubs. Clubheads were formerly made of wood, hence the name. Nowadays, they are made of steel or titanium. Woods are assigned numbers from 1 upwards. Formerly, woods were assigned only 1 to 5. However, the current woods extend as far as 9. The 1 Wood is also called a driver, and it has the lowest loft.

Irons

Irons are clubs used for shorter distances. Their clubheads are made of iron or steel. Irons are also numbered from 1 upwards. As with the woods, the lowest iron has the lowest loft. A standard set of irons consist of numbers 3 to 9.

Golf also includes specialty irons. A Pitching wedge is used to hit a ball high into the air. A Sand wedge is specially designed to play in a sand bunker.

Putters

Putters are clubs designed to send the ball rolling on the ground and into the hole. Therefore, they have no loft. Putters come in all shapes, sizes and lengths. Incidentally, the putter is the only club that can exceed the limit of 48 inches length imposed by the rules.

An experienced golfer knows how far each club hits. You should make it a point to learn this information as well.

Golf Balls for Beginners

As a beginner, you're going to lose a lot of balls - possibly hundreds! You may be surprised how easy it is to lose a ball. Therefore, buying new balls at this point of time is a waste of money.

There are many types of balls you can use when golfing:

Used Balls

No low-handicap golfer wants to be caught playing with a used golf ball. Since you don't belong to that group yet, you won't mind using them. Used balls can be bought at garage sales, pro shops and online.

You should stay away from balls with cuts, bulges or serious discoloration. Because these balls are usually sold in bulk, checking them may pose a problem. Obviously you won't be able to check any online purchases.

Refurbished Balls

Refurbished balls are very good condition used balls. Resellers may repack them into nice boxes. Refurbished balls cost more than used balls found at pro shops.

Closeout Balls

Closeout balls are ones that are no longer produced by the manufacturers. They are either not popular or the manufacturer has decided to concentrate on newer brands. Closeout balls are available online.

Logo Overrun Balls

Many companies purchase in bulk from manufacturers or retailers. Some companies want their logo printed on the balls they order. Logo overrun balls are ones that never make it to the buyers. They are often very high quality name-brand balls. Their prices are lower than new balls of the same brand.

Value Category Balls

Value golf balls are manufactured for high-handicapped golfers. These balls are made differently and behave differently than their higher-ended counterparts. Although these balls are cheaper, they're actually more durable. They're ideal for beginners who insist on playing with new balls.

X-Out Balls

Most big-name companies have high quality control over their production of balls. Balls that don't pass inspection are rejected. Sometimes they're rejected because of a slight smear in the words or minor blemishes. Instead of being destroyed, companies stamp their balls with a row of X's and sell them cheaply.

Is an X-out ball legal? Let's find out.

USGA Decision 5-1/4: Status of an 'X-out' Ball

Q. ' X-out' is the common name used for a golf ball which a manufacturer considers being imperfect and has, therefore, crossed out the brand name on the golf ball. What is the status of an 'X-out' ball?

A. The vast majority of 'X-out' balls are rejected for aesthetic reasons only, i.e., paint or printing errors. In the absence of strong evidence to suggest that an 'X-out' ball does not conform to the Rules, it is permissible for such a ball to be used. However, in a competition where the Committee has adopted the condition that the ball the player uses must be named on the List of Conforming Golf Balls, an 'X-out' ball may not be used, even if the ball in question (without the X's) does appear on the List.

Beginner's Accessories

In addition to a set of clubs and balls, you'll want to purchase other accessories necessary for the game. You should consult the following list:

Bags

A bag is necessary to carry your clubs and a host of other items required on the course. There are 3 types. At this point, you should purchase a carry bag. This is the smallest and easiest to carry around. It's made of lightweight materials and has backpack straps for easier transport. A carry bag may also come with a stand to enable it to stand firmly on the ground. This is called a stand bag.

Note: Seniors golfers shouldn't include more than 9 clubs if they carry their own bags.

Trolleys

Instead of carrying your bag of clubs, you can place it on a trolley. This prevents shoulder strain while still allowing you lots of exercise. There are basically three types of golf trolleys. We suggest the 3-wheeler which is easier to pull or push.

Most trolleys are foldable into a compact size that will fit into the trunk of a car.

Pull: This consists of a metal skeleton frame where you place the bag. At the bottom of the frame, there's a platform for holding the base of your bag. A nylon strap is available to secure the bottom part of your bag. Somewhere higher up are two legs with wheels. Further up the skeleton is a device in the shape of an arc. This holds the top part of the bag and comes with a nylon strap to fasten the bag. At the top of the skeleton is the handle to pull the bag. You can also push it when the terrain is level.

Push: This trolley has all the features of the pull trolley plus an additional wheel, offset at the bottom of the skeleton. This extra wheel enables you to push or pull the trolley with ease. Some models also incorporate a seat. This trolley is especially great for older players.

Electric: The electric trolley is a push trolley with an electric motor attached. This moves the wheels so you don't need to pull or push it. More sophisticated trolleys come with remote controls, stabilizers for steep terrains and even onboard compasses!

Tees

A tee is a small peg with one sharpened end and the other shaped like a dish to hold your golf ball. Tees can be made of wood, plastic or fibers. Golf tees come in all shapes and sizes. The diagram shows some common and not so common tees.

The function of a tee is to elevate your golf ball above the ground. This gives you a better angle to hit the ball farther. Different clubs require different tee heights.

Golf Shoes

Although not a necessity, we advise wearing golf shoes. These special shoes come with spikes or studs which grip the ground firmly. They help you maintain your balance while you swing.

You should purchase waterproof golf shoes so that your feet will remain dry if you play in the rain.

Ball Markers

You don't need to buy ball markers. Any small flat object such as a coin can serve as a marker. In fact, you can even use your golf club to mark your ball.

You mark your ball so that you can pick it up for cleaning or identification and return it to the correct place.

Attire

Always find out whether the club or course you are playing has a dress code. Collared shirt, slacks, socks and shoes will pass most dress codes for men. For the ladies, polo shirt, knee-length shorts, culottes, or pants, socks and shoes are usually acceptable. Wear a cap or hat for good measure.

Gloves

Gloves protect your hands from getting blisters and help you grip the club. The problem is they also take away the feel. Golf gloves are usually made of Cabretta leather or synthetic. Cabretta gloves are softer, but less durable and more expensive. They are also not water-resistant. Synthetics are more durable and waterproof as well as cheaper.

You can certainly play without gloves. Almost all pros remove their gloves when putting.

Golf Umbrella

An umbrella comes in very handy when you are caught in a sudden downpour in the middle of the fairway. It also provides shade from the hot sun.

Umbrellas with huge shades are made especially for golfing. They can provide ample shade for two people – you and your caddie.

Golf Towel

You should always carry a towel with you on the course. You can purchase a golf towel or bring a regular one from home.

These are the basic accessories for a beginning golfer. There are many other golf accessories which you will read about later.

GUIDE TO GOLF LESSONS

There is no substitute for a real-life golf instructor. Here are some benefits that you cannot obtain by reading golf books or watching instructional videos:

- The most immediate danger for a beginner without a golf instructor is learning incorrectly. The golf swing may look simple because the pros often make it look easy. Unfortunately, an incorrect swing may also look simple. Once you develop a wrong swing, you are in trouble as it can be very hard to unlearn.

- For a beginner, professionals can teach you the basics correctly the first time which is very important. You can avoid the tedious, and often unsuccessful, retraining of muscles that are set in performing incorrect motions. A starting skill can be as basic as learning how to grip the club.

- A professional instructor can detect minor errors in your swing and correct them before they become worse. He can also determine the best method of overcoming a physical problem when executing your swing.

- By videotaping your swing, a professional instructor can analyze and point out exactly where you went wrong. This allows you to concentrate on correcting that particular motion instead of relearning everything. Unfortunately, this isn't the case if you use video lessons on your own.

- During an on-course lesson, your instructor can teach you what to do in a given situation such as playing an escape shot from the rough. Unlike a simulation, you'll actually play the shot. You can feel exactly what it's like to hit the shot. This is much more effective.

After receiving lessons from a professional instructor, you may notice different things when you read a golf book or watch a golf video again. This is because you're seeing things in a new light and interpreting information differently. This time, you'll be able to get more out of reference material such as a book or video.

Books and videos have an advantage – they're always available when needed!

Types of Golf Lessons

You can't become a professional golfer in one day. In fact, you won't become a pro in one year. You'll require practice and plenty of it.

Just remember that wrong practice is worse than no practice. You may develop muscle memory for a set of incorrect muscles. Once muscle memory is set, it's very difficult to undo. We have emphasized this many times before. It's better to learn the basics correctly before committing yourself to practicing.

So what should you do? Take lessons.

You need to consider two main options:

- *Day clinics or 2-3 day golf school*

- *Private one-on-one lessons spread over week or months*

Day Clinic

You need to be realistic. One day is not enough time to assimilate all the information required by a beginner. Therefore, day clinics are better suited to golfers who want to perfect a particular skill.

Multiday Clinic Schools

This is a good place to start if you want to learn the basics without too much hassle. You can fit a weekend in to your busy timetable and receive a lot of instruction. Golf schools are also a great way to spend a golf vacation.

Look for schools with a low student-teacher ratio.

As in a day clinic, instructors won't provide follow-up once you leave the school.

Private Lessons

If you have the time and money, a private one-on-one program is the best option. Your coach can monitor your progress. He will know whether you have practiced what he has taught you during the previous lessons.

For a private lesson of this nature to work well, you need a good rapport with your instructor. Therefore, choose your coach carefully.

Basically, there are 3 types of private one-on-one lessons programs:

- A fixed basic program will teach you one or more lesson each session until all the basics are learned.

- An on-going program will allow the coach to build upon the last session. This program is best suited to the serious golfer.

- A one-time lesson caters to golfers who want to learn, improve or correct a particular skill. This lesson usually takes less than 1 hour with the coach.

Before Taking Golf Lessons

Golf lessons can be costly. Before spending your hard-earned money, you should consider the following:

Time

The best lesson is useless if you don't continue to practice on your own. If you don't use it, you will lose it. You'll require lots of practice. Take into consideration how much time you intend to spend practicing after taking the lesson.

Do you plan to be a social golfer or do you want to compete in club tournaments? The harder your goal, the more practice time you will need to achieve it.

Money

Know your budget. Some lessons will cost no more than the price of a lunch. Others may set you back a small fortune.

Instructors who are affiliated with exclusive clubs or establishments tend to charge more. Instructors with a list of famous names displayed on their certificates usually charge a lot more. You may end up paying more for the facilities, not the lessons themselves.

Expensive doesn't necessary mean high quality. You can find many inexpensive teaching professionals who are still very good.

Ask Around

A golf instructor's past students are often his best advertisement.

If you ask a lot of golfers, you'll tend to hear the same names repeated. These names may be recommendations or condemnations, depending on the instructor.

One thing to keep in mind is the instructor's ability to coach beginners.

Talk To Your Potential Coach

Before you commit yourself, talk to the person offering the lessons. Obtain as much information as possible. Does he include video instruction? Will he take you on the course? Has he coached seniors previously?

You should have a list of prepared questions. Discuss your goals and your problems. Your interview will also give you an idea of the rapport between the two of you. Is he a willing listener? If not, search for another instructor. One-way communication won't be very helpful.

Don't Look Back

Once you have made your decision, don't look back. Remain committed to your coach and be prepared for a new learning experience.

Beware of Self-Appointed Gurus

Now that you have the necessary clubs, you may want to visit a driving range to practice hitting on your own. I'm sure you'll be excited about this new adventure and maybe even a bit nervous. This is a good sign that shows you're interested.

Unless you're extremely talented, be prepared to make lots of mistakes and spray balls all over the place. You may become overly conscious of people watching you make a fool of yourself. Try not to worry as every beginner experiences this awkward stage.

You may meet a lot of people at the range who, after seeing your terrible performance, will want to teach you how to play. These self-appointed gurus may be just slightly better than you. You should take their words of wisdom very cautiously. Following their advice could hurt your basics. On the other hand, not following their advice may offend them.

Out of respect, you'll probably follow their advice. Who knows, you may even improve on your swing that day. With a little luck, you may have been offered valuable advice. Just don't commit to that swing until you receive proper golf lessons from a professional.

Books & Videos

Many golf books provide lessons. Videos can teach you everything from a simple swing to the most technical shot-making escapes. On-line lessons will provide step by step instructions with animated video aids. The wide variety of sources may overwhelm you. You can also watch professionals on TV. If possible, record them so you can playback the games in slow motion. After watching a professional on TV, you may think that golf is an easy sport. Rest assured it's not. Professionals spend hours every day practicing. They also have personal coaches to assist them. These all are great to reinforce your lessons by a pro.

PLAYING THE GAME

Proper Warm-Up

DISCLAIMER: Use these exercises we recommend at your own risk. It is recommended that, before beginning any exercise program, individuals seek advice from their physician or a certified exercise professional. The exercises and stretches listed on this web site should be done slowly and carefully. If you feel pain or discomfort STOP IMMEDIATELY!

Never play golf without first warming up your body and loosening your muscles.

Below is a list of the areas you need to warm-up:

If you are pressed for time and some parts of your body are already stretched, choose the particular drill you need.

Shoulder

Standing upright with your legs slightly bent:

- Try to touch your left shoulder with your right elbow to feel the stretch

- Do the same with your left elbow

Chest

Standing upright with your legs slightly bent:

- Hold hands behind your back and keep them straight

- Lift your arms upwards until you feel the stretch across your chest

- Hold for a few seconds

Triceps

Standing upright with feet shoulder width apart:

- Raise your left hand above your shoulder to touch the middle of your back

- Push your left elbow backwards until you feel a stretch at the back of your left arm

- Repeat movement, switching hands

Lower Back

Lying on your back:

- Bend your knees until you can clasp your shins

- Pull your knees until you feel your lower body stretching

Hamstring

Standing upright before a bench, rail or step:

- Put your left leg straight up the bench

- Lean body forward slowly until you feel the stretch in your thigh

- Hold steadily for 5 seconds

- Lean body forward further to stretch more

- Hold steadily for 5 seconds

- Return to upright position

- Repeat motion with right leg on bench

Calf

Standing upright with hands on your hips:

- Bend your right leg forward and extend your left leg behind keeping your knee straight

- Slowly move your hips forwards while keeping your left leg firmly on the ground to feel the stretch

- Hold for 8 seconds

- Switch leg positions and repeat

Standing Lunge

Standing upright with legs hip-width apart:

- Step forward with your left foot and sink down causing your other knee to sink down as well

- Put body weight on heel of your front foot

- Return upright

- Repeat movement, switching legs

Diagonal Lunge

Standing upright with legs hip-width apart:

- Step your left leg forward at 45° and sink down causing your other leg to sink down as well

- Put body weight on front foot

- Return upright

- Repeat movement, switching legs

Squats

Stand upright with legs slightly bend and hip-width apart. Keeping your back straight and your hands on your hips:

- Bend your knees slowly keeping your body angle parallel to your shins and your heels firmly on the floor

- Hold for 3 seconds

- Return upright slowly

- Repeat movement a few times

Holding the Golf Club

Note: Instructions are shown for right-handed golfers. Left-handed golfers should reverse hands.

Many swing inconsistencies are the direct result of an incorrect grip. Your hands are the only connection to the club so you need to grip it properly. A proper grip helps you maintain better control of the clubface on impact. Your hands and your club must work together as a single unit.

You probably started off with the most common overlapping grip. However, it won't hurt to experiment with the two other grips. You may find a grip more suited to your particular style of play. A word of advice: after trying out all three types choose one grip and stick with it.

Many beginners make the mistake of holding the club with the palm of their left hand. This hinders wrist action and reduces power. Placing the club in your fingers increases wrist action. This results in a better feel and more power.

Here's one way to grip the club:

Hold the club with the fingers of your left hand so that the butt end of the club is resting against the fleshy pad of the top of your palm. Using your left hand only, swing the club back to the top of your backswing. Your grip is correct if your left thumb is directly under the shaft, supporting its weight.

Return the club to the initial position. Now open your right hand and gently grip the club below your left hand with your first three fingers. Close your thumb until it almost touches your forefinger. If you close your pinky, you will find it resting between the space between the forefinger and middle finger of your left hand.

You now have the **overlapping grip** which is the most popular. This grip is also called the **Vardon grip**, after Harry Vardon, the great British champion. It's used by most professional golfers. There is more unity because the pinkie of your right hand rests on your left hand. This grip requires strong hands as fewer fingers contact the club.

The Interlocking Grip – The interlocking grip unites both hands as one solid unit. It requires less strength to swing than the overlapping grip and is

suitable for ladies and golfers with smaller hands.

The method of holding this grip is the same as the overlapping grip except that the pinkie of your right hand and the index finger of your left hand are interlocked.

The Interlocking Grip has gained popularity thanks to Tiger Woods.

Whichever style you use, remember to hold your club just tightly enough to control it. Too tight a grip will create tension and restrict your swing. Too loose a grip and your club will move, resulting in errant shots. The rubbing movement will also cause blisters.

The third grip, called the **ten-finger** or **baseball grip**, is one where your fingers neither overlap nor interlock. It's rarely used because your hands don't work as a unit. However, people with very small hands may find it suitable. This grip is quite strong. With all 10 fingers in contact with your club, this grip is firmer than the other two. It allows you more wrist freedom. Because this grip doesn't allow your hands to work as a unit, it's not as popular.

Hold the butt end of the club with your left hand. Then hold the club below your left hand so that both hands touch and all your knuckles line up under the shaft.

The most important thing to remember is not to strangle the club. Your grip should be light. A tight grip creates tension which restricts the fluid movement necessary for a good swing. Test out different grips. Continue experimenting with their positioning until you find one that is both comfortable and effective.

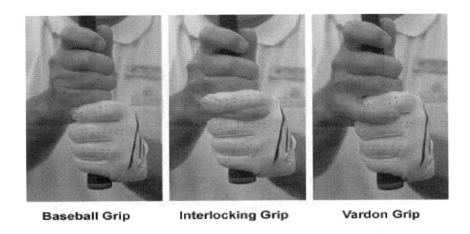

Baseball Grip   **Interlocking Grip**   **Vardon Grip**

Take a closer look at the golf tips later in this book, especially the ones dealing with the correct grip.

Favor a Strong Grip

If your ball continues to fade all the time, chances are you have a weak grip. Your grip is weak if you see no knuckles or only one knuckle on your left hand.

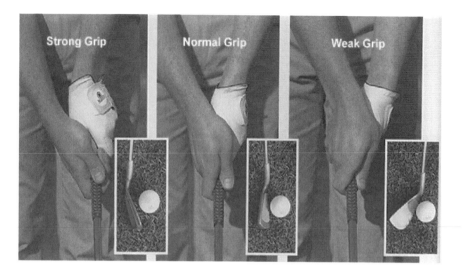

A weak grip weak doesn't release the club enough to square the clubhead at impact. To square the clubhead, a golfer has to consciously rotate his hand counter-clockwise upon impact to produce the squared contact. Conscious actions are never consistent.

It's better to start off with a strong grip where you can see 2-3 knuckles. Another way to determine a strong grip is to look at the V formed by your left hand. It should point to your right shoulder.

With this grip, your hands will automatically rotate upon impact ensuring a square impact. Your ball will fly lower and straighter and may even produce a draw!

The Square Set-Up

The square set-up is the foundation of all golf swings. Without this foundation, your game may be shaky and lack direction. Learning this set-up is quite easy. The only problem is, once you learn it, you may become nonchalant and forget to check on it during a round.

Here's how to adopt the square set-up:

Ball Positions

The diagram on the left provides a simplified idea of the relative ball positions for a driver from the wedges and the positions of your feet. Each circle approximates a golf ball's distance.

Positioning the ball over the various distances of the stance for various club-lengths – back in the stance for wedges and forward for long irons – is a myth. Your left hand can't change position to another part of your body. Since your hand directs the clubface, you can only hit the ground at one spot.

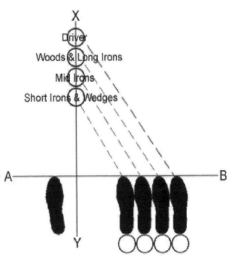

That spot is located approximately 2.5 inches inside your left foot and lies on a line (XY) perpendicular to your line of alignment (AB). This is the location of the lowest part of the club's swing where you want the club to hit the ball. This is also where you want your clubface to be square with the target line.

How far away from the ball should you stand?

This is determined by the length of the club you use. The best way is to place the clubface flush on the ground and let the length of the shaft guide you to your position. Naturally, this shaft should be in line with XY.

How Far Apart?

Regarding the width of your stance, how far apart should you stand?

You can stand with your feet shoulder-width apart and use that distance for all the clubs. However, since a wide stance can restrict your body turn for shorter clubs, a narrower stance is used. This narrower stance is achieved by moving your right foot closer to your left foot. This gives the impression that the ball is moving towards the back of the foot.

The relative position of the right foot movement is one ball width for each range of clubs as shown in the above diagram.

The actual width of the stance varies from person to person. The accepted stance is shoulder width for the long irons, but this isn't always the case. Since your body structure is unique, you should find your own optimum stance width.

You can actually start off with any width and make adjustments from there. Swing with your favorite club. Adjust this width until you are comfortable and consistent. Once you have determined this stance width, you just need to move your right leg closer or farther in relation to that club. The standard movement is one-ball width for each range of clubs as shown in the above diagram.

The best stance is when you feel relaxed and stable. Your stance must enable you to remain balanced after your swing.

The following guidelines will help you build a good stance:

1. Stand with your legs apart at should-width

2. Rotate your left leg slightly towards the target for more stability

3. Keep your right leg perpendicular to the target line

4. Flex your knees slightly

5. Keeping your back straight, jut your buttocks back & tilt your spine forward

6. Move your body weight forward so that your weight is resting on the front of your foot

7. Rest the sole of your clubhead flat on the ground squarely behind the ball

Alignment

You can have the best swing in the world. But if your alignment isn't right, your ball won't reach your target.

The best method to set up your alignment is to visualize a railroad track. Look at the target and form a line to your ball. This is your target line and it forms one of the tracks. The other track is where you stand with your feet, hips and shoulders in line with it.

On the driving range, practice this drill. Place a ball on the ground or mat. Then place a club right behind the ball. This is your target line and one side of the railroad track.

Next, lay a club parallel to your target line. You may need to adjust the distance between these 2 parallels to suit your club.

Now stand behind your club with your toes almost touching the club. Make sure your knees, hips and shoulders are in line with the club on the ground.

When you perform your backswing, your club should move along the line of the yard stick as far as your body will allow.

This practice will help you realize what a square alignment feels like. Once your muscles remember this feeling, you'll be able to align yourself without visual aids.

Posture

A square set-up is one where the toes of your feet form a line parallel to the target line just like a pair of railroad tracks. After making sure your legs are in line, you should check your posture. Good posture is essential to maintain balance.

Here are 7 checkpoints for good posture:

1. Your weight should be evenly distributed on the balls of your feet.

2. Bend from the waist, not the back. Your spine should remain relatively straight.

3. Don't tuck your chin against your chest.

4. Flex your knees – if you look directly down, your knee should be over the middle of your foot.

5. Hang your arms down naturally. The butt of the club should be just a fist away from your body.

6. Put your clubhead down so that the head is aligned squarely with the ball.

7. For a senior golfer, turn your front foot slightly to point at the target to help you turn your body.

The importance of having a square set-up can't be overemphasized. Without it, your shots will be inconsistent. You may hit a good shot now and then, but it may be a matter of two wrongs making a right. Everything will be left to chance.

There are many variables in the game of golf. It's often difficult to determine what went wrong. The only way may be through the process of elimination.

If your set-up is square and your clubhead is square to your target line, your shot should be straight. If your ball doesn't go straight, your swing is to blame, not your set-up. See, you have already eliminated one variable.

Strive to hit a straight shot using the square set-up. Once you have mastered this technique, you can progress to other shot making.

Pre-Shot Routine

A lot has been said about having a pre-shot routine.

- Do you have one?

- If you have one, does it actually work?

If you don't have a pre-shot routine, it's time to start. If you have one already, you can always work on refining it.

Have you ever encountered any of the following?

- Waiting for the group in front to move out of range before you could play?

- Hurried to play faster because people at the back were waiting?

- Waiting in a shelter for a sudden shower to stop?

Such situations tend to disrupt the pace and tempo of your game. Having a pre-shot routine will help to offset such a disruption.

Developing your pre-shot routine may take a while. Give yourself time to plan. Make sure you feel comfortable and confident. Be sure your routine includes all the important details.

You may have copied a pre-shot routine from the pros or from a skilled golfer you admire at your club. If so, it's time for you to develop a new one. For a pre-shot routine to be effective, it must suit *you*. Your type of game, pace and temperament all come into consideration when creating a pre-shot routine.

A mental game consultant states that 3 factors contribute to a good pre-shot routine: a physical signal, an intermediate target and a deep breath.

- Start your routine with a physical gesture. Making a few practice swings is not helpful unless you're going to mirror that during your real swing. Neither is wiping sweat from your brow or flicking away your cigarette. Forget these meaningless gestures and think of something special. I start my pre-shot routine by tapping my club on the ground twice.

- Next, look for an intermediate target. A mark on the ground, a discolored blade of grass or an old divot hole will do. This target shouldn't be farther than 2-3 feet from your ball and on a line between the target and your ball. This can be difficult, especially if the fairway is well mowed.

- This intermediate target will help to improve your alignment. Keep your eyes focused on the intermediate target as you move over to make your swing.

- Make sure your legs, knees and shoulders are in line and parallel to the target line.

- Take a deep breath. This is the final move before commencing with your takeaway for your backswing. Make sure your entire body is relaxed.

Remember the 3 steps of your pre-shot routine the next time you tee-off.

Club First Set-Up

First you stand behind the ball and look at the target, and then you choose an intermediate target. Having done that, you align your feet parallel to the target line made by the ball and the intermediate target line. The next step is to align your clubface so that it's square to the ball and target line.

The above procedure is fine. However, most golfers are reluctant to move from their position for fear of stepping out of line once they plant their feet firmly on the ground. Instead, they move their clubs.

When you address the ball first and then the club, you can't gauge how far away from the ball you should position yourself. Since your legs and ball are already in place, two things can happen.

- If the ball is slightly too far away, you may hunch over to reach it. This will leave your clubface in a toe-up position.

- If the ball is too close, you may stand too erect, resulting in a clubface that is toe-down.

To avoid these two positions, start by setting the club down before lining your feet. This allows you to set your clubface flush with the ground and then let the length of the club determine your distance.

Below is a step-by-step procedure you can practice to perfect your set-up:

1. Place a club on the ground with its butt almost touching the ball. Position the club so that it's perpendicular to the target line. This is your reference club.

2. Place the club you're using to hit the ball behind the ball so that its head is flush with the ground.

3. Keeping the clubhead on the spot, step over your reference club with your front foot (left for a right-hander) so that it's about 2.5 inches from your reference club. This is the normal distance where the clubface will make contact with the ground. Your front foot should remain in this position.

4. With your front foot set, move your hands so that they are properly lined up with the club.

5. Move your back foot behind to suit the club you are using. You're now properly set up to hit the ball. Refer to the Square Stance for relative ball positions.

After some time, you should practice the same set up without the reference club on the ground. You should be able to visualize it and position your body accordingly.

The Intermediate Target

Now you know what to do. Club first, then body. You see the target and you visualize the line from the target to your ball. You picture the railroad track - you need to align your body on the other track. You place your club and start walking to the other track.

Hey! What happened to the track? The target line has mysteriously disappeared!

You go back behind the ball and start over. The target line disappears again.

Why? Because the target is so far away.

Go behind that ball and visualize the target line again. Pick an object such as a twig or leaf that is 1-2 feet in front of the ball. This is called the intermediate target. When you return to the address position, you'll still see that intermediate target and draw a line from it to the ball. Now stand squarely to that line.

Practice Check

This is a good practice habit whenever you go to the range. Just like the square set-up, alignment can deteriorate due to complacency.

Even with the intermediate target, you may find you're not standing squarely to it. A slight offset in your alignment and the ball will completely miss your target. Therefore, it's essential that you get your alignment correct for each address.

You can't use an artificial aid or move anything natural as an alignment aid during a round of golf. However, you should use an aid if you're practicing on the range or on your own. The easiest aid is another golf club.

Find a distant target you are supposed to hit, and then visualize your target line. Find your intermediate target and determine your stance from there. Once you have firmly got your address and are ready to swing, stop.

Instead of swinging, put the club you're holding on to the ground. Line it up so that it touches both your toes. This is your feet alignment. Now take another club and lay it down so that it touches the ball and your intermediate target. This is your target line. Now walk behind both your clubs.

Are these two clubs parallel? If so, your alignment is correct.

If not, practice until they are. Practice this procedure until you get the feel of it.

The Swing

Now we come to the third and most important technique – the swing.

This is the bread and butter of the game. Everyone strives for the "Perfect Golf Swing". Some say it's just a myth. A perfect golf swing is one that enables you to consistently hit the ball exactly where you want it to go. It's doubtful that a human can do that. The good news is you can come close with enough practice.

There are 3 parts to a swing: the Backswing, Downswing and Follow-through.

The Backswing

Every swing begins with the backswing. You initiate your backswing with your body, NOT your hands. To start the backswing, you perform what is called the "takeaway". The take-away starts with the body. When your body turns to the right, your shoulders, arms and hands will follow. During this stage, try to keep both arms straight and relaxed. Many high-handicap golfers, including some professionals, begin their takeaway by lifting their clubs from the ground. This slight upward motion disrupts the smooth slow of the backward motion.

A better method is to start with the club above ground level. Most professionals waggle their clubheads before taking them backwards. This loosens your muscles and triggers the starting motion. It's similar to the cocking of a gun.

Start with your shoulder. As your shoulder turns, your arms and hands must follow as a unit. Try to keep both hands straight and relaxed. Your right elbow will start to break when the club's shaft is in line with your feet. Your club will then travel upwards. At the point when the shaft is parallel to the ground, your clubhead should be pointing towards the sky.

At the highest point, your right elbow should be 90 degrees and the club shaft should remain parallel to the ground. Your weight should be on your right foot and your chin should touch your left shoulder.

The Downswing

Maintaining a slight pause at the top of the backswing before making your move downwards is a good technique.

The downswing brings the clubface within contact of the ball at the desired speed of the golfer. This is called the "controlled speed". Whatever speed you want to generate must be under your control. This is often easier said than done. Even world class professionals sometimes force their swings beyond their control.

Your left foot initiates the downswing. Roll your left foot to the outside to signal a weight shift from right to left. This shift is accompanied by turning just your shoulder, not your entire body. Don't lift your head up and focus on the ball.

You should treat the path of the downswing as the exact reverse of the backswing. Only this time, the speed is faster. As you approach impact, your arms and hips should return to their original position. This is very important in bringing the clubface back to a square position. Your eyes must remain focused on the ball at all times. As your clubhead reaches the impact area, your arms should pull you through the shot. Upon impact, your weight transfer continues until all your weight is on your left foot.

The Follow-Through

Don't stop your club the moment you hit the ball. The natural momentum of your swing will carry you and your club further. Your hips continue the pivoting motion, pulling your right leg off the ground. Your shoulders, hips and right knee should all point towards the target. Your chin should be resting on your right shoulder.

The basic golf swing isn't very difficult to learn. Once you have mastered the following pointers, you should develop a proper swing and hit the ball straight:

- Use the correct grip

- Maintain a stable and proper stance

- Align to the target

- Keep your feet firmly on the ground

- Keep your left arm straight

- Push in your backswing

- Pull through your downswing

- Follow through

- Have a smooth swing

- Keep your eyes on the ball

- Practice

Again, please take a closer look at the tips and lessons section later in this book for more detailed advice.

Practice Swing & Actual Swing

Beginners always feel like Tiger Woods when they perform their practice swing. However, the actual swing is something completely different.

Why?

We call it mental 'overloading'.

When you take your practice swing, you are performing this action without a ball. You are just getting the feel of the swing that you're about to take. The moment you step up to the ball, you see an extra object. This places extra pressure on your brain and nervous system and may cause mental overload.

You may have heard the saying 'the ball just happens to be on the path of your normal swing'. You are supposed to swing as if the ball isn't there. This is often easier said than done.

So is there a solution?

Fortunately, there is a solution, but it's not immediate.

Instead of swinging at air during your practice swing, focus on an object such as a blade of grass or some earth. Then step up and swing at a similar object.

Your system overloads because of the lack of muscle memory relating to the relevant skill. You rarely see pro golfers in a tournament taking practice swings. That's because they don't need to. They already know what it takes to perform the swing. Therefore, they can focus their attention elsewhere.

Think back to when you were young and learning to drive a car with manual gear shifts. There were so many things to consider. You had to remember to step on the accelerator, step on the clutch and then shift the gear while keeping your other hand on the steering wheel. Suddenly you see a car in front and panic. You jam on the brakes, or worse, you forget where the brakes are and hit the accelerator! Now that you're an experienced driver, you're calmer because your body knows exactly what to do.

The swing scenario is very similar. Once you have developed muscle memory, you won't need to worry about that small white round object in front of you. Developing muscle memory will take time. Just make sure you develop the correct muscle memory.

Steps for a Smooth Swing

You may wonder how professionals can send their balls so far and so effortlessly, when you practically jump out of your socks. This is exactly the problem. Brute strength won't send your ball far.

What you want is a smooth swing. This reminds me of a question my physics teacher asked when teaching the flow of water. "Which has more energy; streamline flow or turbulent flow?" We pictured the powerful foaming water over rocks and answered a turbulent flow. "Wrong", my teacher said expectantly. "Energy is converted into heat in turbulence. In streamline motion, there is no conversion." This analogy reminds me of a smooth swing with no loss of energy.

Below are six steps to achieve the smooth swing characteristic of the pros:

1. **Light grip** - Imagine the tension flowing out of your arms. Your grip should be likened to clasping a small bird. With your arms relaxed, you should be able to swing your club back in a smooth, wide arc.

2. **Lively Legs** – Think of your legs as two coiled springs. Bounce a little as you flex your knees when addressing the ball. Ensure the

weight of your body is moving on to your right leg in your backswing. Do not make the transition until you feel the entire weight on your right leg.

3. **Wide Arc** – Your torso should lead your backswing. Now visualize your left arm and the club fused together. Swing this unit slowly and smoothly back, making a wide arc around your spine. The wider the arc, the farther your clubhead. This distance provides the momentum for a faster swing.

4. **Legs First** – Many short hitters swing with their upper body only. To get more power, use your entire body. Start the chain reaction with your left leg. Your left leg rolls outside toward the target, bringing your lower body to start the turn. Now you must transfer your body weight on to your left leg. This will pull your arms and hands into impact with increasing speed.

5. **Swing Through** – Concentrate on your swing along the target line as your right hand overtakes your left at the follow-through. Concentrating on your swing instead of the ball will eliminate the tendency to steer the clubhead. Steering is one of the main factors in reducing swing speed. Complete your swing - the poor ball just happens to be in the way.

6. **High Finish** – Imagine your hands above your head, your clubhead behind you, your weight on your left foot and your belly button slightly left of the target in the finish position. In order to achieve this beautiful finish, you must swing smoothly through impact without steering the clubhead.

That Left Arm Controversy

How many times have you heard the advice "Keep your left arm straight"?

You may have tried it out and find you're still topping or slicing the ball.

Let's digress a little.

Miller Barber was born on March 31, 1931. He probably learned the game by himself during his younger days. That was because he had a quirky swing. He would swing his club back to the outside and stick it straight up as if he was trying to open an umbrella. A lot of golfers found this hilarious. Barber's funny swing has won him 11 tournaments on the regular Tour and 24 on the Senior Tour, including 3 US Senior Opens!

When Calvin Peete, born July 18, 1943, was 12 years old he climbed up a cherry tree at his grandmother's house. He reached out for a branch and it broke. He fell to the ground and shattered his left elbow. Surgeons repaired the elbow, but it remained permanently fused. Peete could never fully straighten his arm again. At the age of 23, he picked up the game of golf. With his bent arm, he became a professional golfer in 1971. From 1979 to 1986, he won 11 PGA Tour events. Peete's bent arm helped him earned the nickname "Mr. Accurate".

The point of the above stories: "You don't need to keep your left arm straight."

Keeping it straight upon impact is what matters. What happens before or after is immaterial.

Having said that, playing with a straight left arm will lead to a more consistent swing and straighter ball flight.

Actually, most healthy golfers won't find it difficult to keep their left arm fairly straight throughout the backswing. Then what is the reason for your problem?

Actually there are two reasons:

First, you try to move your arms and hands farther around than your torso has turned. Once your torso has stopped turning, your left arm should also stop. The most you should allow is a little lifting. Your arms should face the same direction as your chest at the top of your backswing, not wrapped around your neck or behind your back.

Try this test in your own room:

- With a club in your hands, stand upright in front of a mirror.

- Stretch your arms straight out in front of you. The club shaft should be pointing straight up at the ceiling.

- Keeping your head steady and facing the mirror, turn your body until your left shoulder is in line with your chin or as close as possible. Your arms should turn together with your body.

- Look at the mirror to see if your arms are still straight and parallel to the ground.

- Tilt your spine toward the mirror and lift your arms slightly.

- This is approximately the top of your backswing position.

Golfers with any flexibility problems should find this movement easy. If you are having difficulty performing this movement, you should consult a golf pro. A bit of stretching can help. Otherwise, you may have to adopt a shorter backswing.

Count Your Cadence

There is nothing like the thrill of giving a mighty whack with your big stick when you tee off. While we get the satisfaction of unleashing our fury on that poor ball, we often end up all over the course instead of the fairway.

Swinging too hard often upsets our timing. This leads to poor contact and inconsistency. You want to swing hard, but you also want to maintain your rhythm. One way to do this is to count your cadence.

Everyone's cadence is different. You can see this on the course itself. Some golfers will be walking briskly, whereas others have a more moderate tempo. A few golfers will be taking their own sweet time during a game.

None of these are right or wrong.

What is suitable for one golfer may not be suitable for another. You have your own tempo, and you should use that tempo when counting your cadence.

There are several ways of counting cadence. Some golfers call words, some use alphabets and others utter sentences. The easiest is to count 1-2-3-4; 1 signifying the moment you start moving your club in your backswing and whatever number you reach on your downswing.

Find your optimum cadence count for the entire swing first.

Let's take the numeric counting for your swing as your example. Preferably, there should be no pause in between each number. A count of 1---2---3-456 will not do. Instead, it should be 1-2-3-4-5-6-7-8.

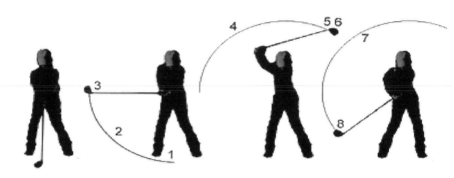

Once you've established the timing of your cadence and the number you reached for your downswing, you can break up each part of your swing with this cadence.

Your takeaway should be slow like 1-2-3 with 3 being the position of your clubhead when your body is fully coiled. The move up to the top of your backswing should be 4-5. Preferably, you will need a slight pause at the top 6-7. The 8 will be your move down and 9 will be your impact.

The above cadence count may not reflect yours. But you can see that it's a swing controller. If you find that your backswing has reached the top on 4 instead of 5, you're swinging too fast.

The cadence count shouldn't make you swing in parts. Your swing should be smooth, but should reach the appropriate check-points of the count in its motion.

Once you master this cadence count, you can be assured that every swing will be smooth.

Driving Range Practice

As a beginner, you should practice at a driving range instead of a golf course. Even if you have already taken lessons, you need to reinforce what you have learned. The driving range is the best place to accomplish this.

If this is your first time out on the range, here are a few pointers to observe:

1. **Don't Use Your Own Balls.** Never practice with your own golf balls unless you want to donate them to the range. You can't retrieve a hit ball.

2. **Buy Practice Balls.** Purchase practice balls from the range attendant or ball dispensing machine. If you buy them from a machine, hang a bucket on the hook below the ball drop. Once you insert the tokens, the machine will dispense the relevant number of balls.

3. **Choose A Bay.** A driving range has several bays or stalls numbering from 12 to a few dozen. These bays are separated by partitions. Try to choose a bay located far from other golfers so you don't distract them.

4. **Tee Up.** Some driving ranges have automatic ball machines that tee-up your ball if you step on a pedal. Otherwise, you have to manually tee-up.

5. **Synthetic Mats.** Most driving ranges use synthetic mats or artificial grass that has rubber tees for your balls. If there is no tee, insert one into the available holes. Just lift up the mat and insert the tee through the bottom.

6. **Natural Grass.** If you practice on natural grass, you need more room because of the divots you'll create. Don't hit from the exact same spot.

7. **Use All Your Clubs.** Since you are new to the range, practice using all your clubs to get used to the feel of each one. In the latter part of your session, concentrate on one or two clubs to practice your swing.

8. **Don't Show Off.** As you search for an open bay, you may notice a golfer driving his ball really far. Many golfers do this just to impress others. Resist the temptation and concentrate on practicing.

9. **Different From Actual Course.** Be aware that a driving range is never the same as a real golf course. Even with natural grass, they can't simulate a real situation. You always perform better on a range than a golf course because you're more relaxed and you're repeating the same swing. Unfortunately, you don't have this luxury on an actual course.

Now to the practice part:

The driving range is the place to practice your game, shot by shot. Regular practice at the golf driving range will benefit every golfer's game. Having said that, many people don't get the full benefit out of a trip to the range. Quite often people on the driving range just hit one ball after the other, often without looking where the shot went. In my eyes this is a waste of effort.

You should hit your practice shot, look at it, analyze it and make adjustments as needed. This way fewer balls can actually lead to faster progression of the game, and it's also a lot less stressful.

To get you started here are five practice tips for the next time you hit the range:

1. Do not just knock balls into the air for the mere benefit of seeing them fly. Instead, have a goal of exactly what you want out of each session. Decide what you want to achieve and focus on that.

2. Always aim for a target, whether it be someplace on the artificial green, a yardage marker sign, or a patch of grass.

3. Learn when to stop. When you come to the point on the driving range when you have reached your goal for the day, learn when to stop. Hitting too many balls can lead to injury and boredom.

4. Give equal practice time to your short game as you do your long-distance shots.

5. When practicing your short shots, never hit them from the same spot each and every time. Vary your length and distances for faster progression. Also vary the directions so that you are not always aligned the same way.

BASIC GOLF ETIQUETTE

Unlike most sports, the game of golf is played without the supervision of officials or referees. This doesn't mean you can do anything you like. You may be well versed with the rules of the game. However, there's something even more important – golf etiquette.

The essence of golf etiquette is reflected in the official rules:

"The overriding principle is that consideration should be shown to others on the course at all times."

Don't become bogged down by too many rules. Remember you're out to enjoy yourself. Just keep in mind the following guidelines when you're on the course:

Dress Code

Before you visit a course, make sure you know their dress code. Many exclusive clubs impose strict dress codes even if you're not playing golf. Municipal and public courses are more relaxed.

Even if a club or course has no dress code, you should be properly attired. For men, slacks and collared sports shirts will suffice. Ladies should wear knee-length shorts, culottes or pants, a sports shirt and ankle-high socks.

Wear golf shoes, even if they're not required. With the soft studs nowadays, they're just as comfortable as trainers. Golf shoes also offer better traction.

Gloves are a personal option. Some golfers prefer to play without them. Gloves provide a better grip, but they can also hinder feel, especially while putting.

Be Punctual

You need to book a tee time for most public and private golf courses. Once a tee time is reserved, make sure you arrive on time. Try to arrive 30 minutes early.

If you miss the appointed tee time, your group will lose its spot. Another slot may not be available for hours on a busy day.

Tipping

You don't need to tip on a municipal or public course. For other courses, bring extra cash to tip employees providing services such as delivering carts and carrying your bags from your car. Find out about the normal tipping rate. Usually the higher the green fee, the higher the tipping rate.

Avoid Slow Play

More tempers are lost over slow play than any other incident on a golf course.

Nobody likes to be kept waiting. Prepare ahead of your turn. Get the club you're going to use ready. On the green, read your line while others are reading theirs, unless you'll disturb the person about to putt.

If your group is slow, signal for the group to play through. They'll appreciate your show of etiquette. Your group is considered slow if a clear hole is ahead of yours.

Be ready to play as soon as it's your turn. When playing on or near the putting green, leave your bag or cart in such a position that will permit a quick exit to the next tee. Once the play of a hole is finished, immediately leave the putting green.

Ready Golf

Slow play is never acceptable. When you're playing on a busy course or during peak hours, you should ignore the rule formalities and play 'ready golf'.

1. Play the moment you reach your ball.

2. When you know you can no longer score, pick up your ball.

3. Mark your score at the next tee box, not at the green.

4. Signal the group behind you to play through if you're searching for a ball. Play at an estimated position instead of going back. Just remember to add a 2-stroke penalty.

5. Make sure your equipment and cart are close to the next tee box.

6. Concede all "gimmies".

7. Remember, you should be just behind the front group, not just in front of the group behind you.

The above steps can save as much as 3-4 minutes for each hole!

Course Care

Be responsible and take care of the course using the following guidelines:

- When using a cart always observe cart rules and keep your cart on the tracks

- Repair ball marks or pitch marks while on the green. Use a 'divot-tool'.

- Replace or repair divots on the fairway. If you chunk off a piece of divot, replace it immediately. Old divot holes can be repaired by pouring sand or seed into them. Always take a container of sand or seed with you.

- Rake bunkers after you play. Rake and smooth a bunker even if you're not playing in it.

   Note: While playing in a bunker, don't touch the sand during your address.

It's Just a Game

If you miss a two-foot putt and smash your putter on the green, who suffers?

Certainly not your opponents.

Golf can be a very frustrating game. But remember, it's just a game. Getting worked up and raising your blood pressure won't help. Besides being bad for your health, your image will also suffer.

Priority on the Course

Priority on the course is determined by a group's pace of play. Any group playing a whole round is entitled to pass a group playing a shorter round.

Scoring

If you're a marker in stroke play, check the score with the player concerned and record it before or while on the way to the next tee.

Shhh!

The golf ball is a small object. You need full concentration when trying to hit it properly. You don't want any noise to distract you. As a similar courtesy, don't disturb another golfer by moving, talking or making unnecessary noise when he's about to play. You should also turn off distracting electronic devices.

No Blocking

Don't walk or stand in front of someone who is about to play, even if you are 100 yards away. Besides distracting the person, you may endanger yourself!

Green Manners

When on the putting green, never step on the line of your partner's ball. This spoils the ground on his line of putt. Don't cast your shadow over his line of putt. Standing directly behind him while he putts is also considered poor etiquette.

Preventing Damage

Don't remove divots when taking practice swings. Place a stand bag outside the green to prevent damaging it with your bag or flagstick.

Don't stand too close to the hole or use the head of a club to remove a ball from the hole. Always replace the flagstick properly before leaving the putting green.

Safety

A golf ball in flight can be a dangerous thing. Never play until the players in front are out of range. If there are workers nearby, alert them. If you find your ball heading in a direction where it may hit someone, immediately shout the traditional warning. "FORE"!

If you hear this warning, immediately cover your head and face with your arms.

Golf clubs are even more dangerous. Getting hit by a golf club can be fatal.

Make sure nobody is standing near you when you swing. Stones, pebbles or may also be dislodged so be careful.

Knowing and observing golf etiquette will help you become a better golfer.

It may not improve your skill, but it will help you earn the respect of fellow golfers. Golfers prefer to play with partners who practice proper etiquette.

HEALTH AND SAFETY CONCERNS

Though golf is a relatively low-risk game, injuries can occur. Often injuries are the result of carelessness or foolhardiness. Below are some common injuries and how to prevent them:

- **Blisters** – Blisters are caused by friction. The rubbing of the golf club against your hand wears down the skin. To avoid blisters on your hands, use the correct size gloves. You can also get blisters on your feet if you are wearing new or incorrectly sized shoes. Wearing thicker socks can prevent foot blisters.

- **Dehydration** – Playing outdoors in the sun can make your body lose a lot of water and can cause dehydration if the water isn't replaced. Make sure you drink a lot of water before you play and take enough water with you during your rounds. You may also drink soda or any isotonic drinks. Alcoholic drinks will not help.

- **Sunburn** – Although the sunshine can be enjoyable, you risk getting sunburned. Always wear a hat or cap to protect your face from direct sunlight. Apply sunscreen on your arms and to any other exposed parts of your body. Wearing long-sleeved clothing will also help.

- **Insect Bites** – Any vast areas containing grass and water are ideal breeding grounds for insects such as bugs and mosquitoes. Applying insect repellant before starting your round will prevent insect bites.

- **Backaches** – This is the most problematic area for a golfer because of the twisting and turning actions during each swing. To lessen this risk, make sure your muscles are more flexible by adequate warming them up.

- **Lightning** – This is the most dangerous risk. The vast open area of the golf course increases the risk. Your club can also act like a lightning rod. If you're playing in an area prone to lightning, be very careful. Most clubs sound a warning when lightning looms. If you hear this sound, abandon play and head for the clubhouse. There's always another day to play.

RULES OF THE GAME

You must learn the rules when you play golf. Few golfers know every single rule, not even the pros. However, it's imperative that you are familiar with the common rules. Otherwise, you will be a burden to your golf partners.

Knowing the rules puts you in an advantageous position over a person who doesn't know them. You will know that it's legal to clean your ball when it's on the green. You will also realize that you can pull out an embedded ball without incurring a penalty.

The following section explains the basic rules of golf. Try to learn them before your next game.

Equipment Rules

Club

You are allowed to carry a maximum of 14 clubs in your bag, although you may bring less. Make sure you take all the necessary clubs because you aren't allowed to borrow a club from a fellow golfer.

Ball

Make sure you have plenty of golf balls because you'll lose many. It's your responsibility to know which ball you're using. You may pick a ball up for identification anywhere, except in a hazard. The ball must be replaced exactly where you picked it up. Therefore, you have to mark the exact spot before you pick up the ball.

In a tournament, you must play the same ball from the tee to the hole. You may only use another one if your ball is damaged along the way.

Tees

Always take more tees than the number of holes you're playing. You shouldn't be without one when you need it. You may borrow one from a fellow golfer, but this projects a poor image.

Playing Rules

In a tournament, a standard round of golf involves completing 18 holes on a golf course. If a course has only 9 holes, you will have to play twice.

If you're playing recreational golf, you can choose to play nine holes. In fact, we recommend that senior golfers walk 9 holes, instead riding on a cart for 18 holes.

Four-Player Limit

Always try to play in a group. A maximum of 4 players is allowed in a group.

Order of Play

Be ready to tee off when it's your turn. Play the white tees if you're a beginner and the red tees if you're a woman.

On a social round, whoever tees off first is rarely an issue. The main thing is not to waste time. Draw lots to decide who will tee off first on the initial hole. For ensuing tees, the player with the best score on the preceding hole goes first (his "honor"), and so on in ascending order of scores. For golfers who tie, follow the order in the preceding hole.

On the fairway or putting green, the player who is "away" or "out" plays first. These terms refer to the player whose ball is furthest from the hole.

The exception to this rule is when 'ready golf' is being played. In 'ready golf', whoever is ready can play. You'll often see more than one golfer playing at the same time. Golfers play 'ready golf' to speed up the round.

Play As It Lies

You can't move the golf ball in order to improve your shot. Unless you're very well versed with the rules, play the ball as it lies. This is always the safest option.

Many unpleasant arguments arise from players who move their ball to another position. Unless all the golfers in your group are aware of the rule, don't touch the ball. Bear in mind that some players may interpret a rule differently.

The only exception to this rule is on the green. You can pick up your ball on the green in order to clean it. Just make sure to mark the exact spot beforehand.

Ball Marking

As we mentioned before, you can only mark your ball on the green.

Sometimes your marker will interfere with another player's putt. Ask him if he would like you to move your marker, and in which direction. You can then move the marker one clubhead's distance from the original marker. Make sure you replace your ball at the original position. Otherwise, you incur a 2-stroke penalty.

The Flagstick

When your ball is outside the green, you can leave the flagstick in the hole or have it removed. You can't change your mind once your ball is in motion.

When your ball is on the green, the flagstick must be removed from the hole.

Obstructions

If your ball is lying on a natural obstacle such as trees, large rocks or roots, you have to play it where it lies. However, if the obstacle is artificial such as a lawn mower or pipe, you are entitled to relief. Pick up your ball and drop it at the nearest point of relief. Your ball must not be placed closer to the hole.

Loose Impediments

Loose impediments are items such as twigs, stones, leaves or cigarette butts that are scattered around the course. If they interfere with your play, you can clear them. Just be careful not to move your ball in the process. Otherwise, it will cost you one penalty stroke.

Playing the Wrong Ball

Make sure you play with your own ball. Playing a ball other than your own incurs 2 penalty strokes. You have to retrieve your own ball before the next tee-off.

Handicaps

One great thing in golf is the handicap. Handicapping enables all players with different skill levels to have a fair chance of winning.

Most tournament participants require an official handicap before starting. A beginning golfer has to pass a handicap test before receiving his handicap. A more experienced golfer will have a lower handicap than a less skillful player. A professional will have a zero handicap.

When you play a round of golf, there will be two scores: your gross score and your net score. Your gross score is the total number of strokes you require to complete the 18-holes. Your net score is your gross score minus your handicap.

Here are the scores of players A and B:

	A	**B**
Handicap	2	20
Total strokes after 18-holes	95	95
Gross Score	78	95
Net Score	76 (78 – 2)	75 (95 – 20)

The above table indicates that Player A is better than player B because his handicap is lower. After 18 holes, Player A scores 78 and Player B scores 95. However, player B beats A by 1 stroke after his handicap is included.

Par Terms

There are various terms you should know for each hole. The Par number for a hole indicates the total number of strokes a skilled golfer needs to sink his ball.

Here are some other common terms in ascending order:

Condor (Triple Eagle)	Par – 4

Albatross (Double Eagle)	Par – 3
Eagle	Par – 2
Birdie	Par – 1
Par	Par – 0
Bogie	Par + 1
Double Bogie	Par + 2
Triple Bogie	Par + 3

Higher scores are simply called overs, such as 4-over or 5-over. If you consistently score these, return to the driving range for more practice!

Hazards

Out of Bounds (OB)

Boundary markers are defined by white stakes or lines. Your ball is considered out of bounds (OB) if it lands on or outside the lines. If you hit an OB, you incur one penalty stroke. You must return to your last location and hit the ball again.

Lost Ball (LB)

If you hit a ball and can't find it within 5 minutes, you declare a lost ball (LB). One penalty stroke is added to your score and you must return to where you last hit the ball and hit again. If you are searching for a ball, signal the group behind you to play through.

Provisional Ball (PB)

Always play a provisional ball if you think your ball may be lost or out of bounds.

Make sure you let the golfers in your group know you're playing a PB. You may need to play a ball of a different brand or number than the first one.

If you find your first ball in bounds, play it. Your next stroke is your second stroke with no penalty. Otherwise, play your PB. Your next stroke is your fourth stroke with a stroke and distance penalty.

Note: balls lost in a water hazard are treated differently.

Water Hazards

There are numerous rules regarding water hazards depending on the situation.

Normal Hazard

If your ball falls into a normal hazard, take a one-stroke penalty. You can drop another ball near the edge of the water where you think your ball crosses and play from there. Just make sure the ball isn't closer to the hole. If you refuse to pay the penalty, you can enter the water and try to hit your ball out.

Lateral Water Hazard

If your ball falls into a lateral water hazard, you can wade in and try to splash it out without penalty. If you prefer to remain dry, you must pay a one-stroke penalty and drop your ball within one club length from the point it crosses the edge of the water. Your ball must not be closer to the hole.

During dry spells, the water in a water hazard may dry up. Nevertheless, the hazards and rules pertaining to them remain the same.

Unplayable Lie

If you hit your ball into a spot where you just can't take a shot, you can declare it an unplayable lie. This costs you a one-penalty stroke. Measure a distance of 2-clubs length from the ball and drop your ball there. Make sure your ball isn't closer to the hole than it was previously.

You can also draw an imaginary line from the hole to the ball in the unplayable lie. You can extend it backwards as far as you like and drop your ball on that line.

You always have option of returning to where you last played and continuing from there.

Winter Rule

For crazy golfers who brave the cold of winter, one rule allows you to move your ball a few feet from its current location to find a better lie. However, this rule is unofficial.

These are just some of the rules that you should know when you play golf. To learn more, you can visit the official USGA or R&A websites.

Last but not least, please remember that rules can be interpreted in more than one way. It's one thing to know the rules and quite another to argue about them while playing. You're there to enjoy the game. Don't let the rules get in the way and spoil your game.

GOLF COURSES

You may have spent significant time practicing at the driving range and are starting to become bored. There is no one left to impress at the range and even the residential pro nods his head in approval whenever you swing. You're now ready to take your clubs to a golf course!

No two golf courses are exactly the same. This is another reason why golf is so exciting. Serious golfers like to play as many courses as possible.

Types of Golf Courses

Private Golf Courses – Only club members are allowed to play on a private golf course or country club. These courses are very well kept. There are strict protocols and club rules that members must observe.

These clubs are expensive, but you get what you pay for. Some clubs are so exclusive that membership is by invitation only.

Resort Golf Courses - Resort golf courses are usually owned by high class hotels or holiday resorts. They can range from mediocre to world class and are available to guests at a decent price. They may also be available to non-hotel guests for a higher price.

Daily Fee Golf Courses – These are semi-private courses. The clubs are open to the public who pays a day fee. Some of these clubs have members like the private clubs. Such clubs impose restrictions on the public regarding playing days or times.

Municipal Golf Courses – A municipal golf course is open to local residents. Non-residents are permitted to play at a higher price. This course offers the best value for money. Some municipal courses are exclusively for local residents.

Public Golf Courses – A public golf course is open to anybody willing to pay for a round of golf. This type of course is the cheapest. Because of the lower price, they tend to be crowded, especially during weekends and holidays. You will need to book in advance if you want to play.

Beginner's Course – There is also a course that caters to beginners like you. A beginner's, or executive course, is short and usually consists of nine par-3 holes, with an occasional easy par-4. Because these courses are relatively easy, they are seldom frequented by skilled players. You may meet players who are worse than you. A beginner's course is a great place to build your confidence.

Choosing a Golf Course

With so many different golf courses available, it may be hard to decide. Here are a few pointers to help you make the right choice:

Cost

Depending on the size of your wallet and your personal preference, you can choose the inexpensive public courses or purchase a membership to an exclusive private golf club. You'll be able to rub shoulders with the town's elite while enjoying immaculate greens and gleaming fairways. An exclusive private golf club doesn't necessary equate to really experienced golfers. On the contrary, you may encounter very skilled golfers in semi-private clubs.

Course Difficulty

You're still considered a rookie despite your experience at the driving range. Remember, the golf course is completely different than a driving range.

As a beginner, you want some challenges so you don't become bored. However, you don't want too many difficult challenges or you'll want to give up after a few holes. Choose a course that poses some challenges, but ones you can handle.

Course Rating & Slope

Most golf courses have two numbers to describe their difficulty. The first number is called the course rating. This number shows the average score a "scratch golfer" will need to play 18 holes. This number is usually between 67 and 77.

The second number is the slope. The course slope shows the difficulty of the course for a "bogey golfer". The easiest course has a slope number of 55, while the most difficult has a slope of 155. The higher the slope number, the more difficult the course. The average slope is 113.

Location & Conditions

Most golfers prefer to play nearby courses. Playing conditions are also important. Do you prefer to play in a very calm region or where there is wind? The grass may differ on each course. Playing on different courses prepares you to face various conditions and situations. This makes you a more well-rounded player.

Pace of Play

Public courses are usually crowded during the holidays. You will have to play faster because people are waiting. If you want a more relaxed, leisurely pace, you have to play on a less crowded day or at a more expensive course.

Golf Course Map

You can get lost on a golf course! You don't want to waste time wondering which direction to take. To help you find your way around, every golf course includes a map. Maps are often located near the club house or on the course's scorecards.

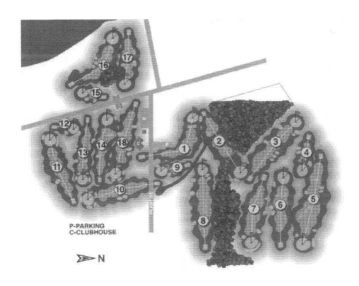

P-PARKING
C-CLUBHOUSE

➤ N

Course maps can be very simple like the one above or very detailed. Use the map to find your way around the course. It may prove useful in an emergency when you need to find shelter or answer the call of nature.

Typically a course map shows you the following details:

- Location of tee boxes, fairways, hazards, greens and holes

- Location of the clubhouse, snack bars, restrooms, shelters, service areas and pathways

Hole Pars

A standard golf round consists of 18 holes. These holes are not equal distance. Some are short, whereas others are quite long. You can see the length of each hole at the tee box. A board is always available to show you all the information for that hole. The information includes the hole number, par number, index number and the distance from the various tees.

Here is typical data for a hole: Hole 12, Par 5, Index 6, Black 526 yards, Blue 505 yards, White 489 yards, and Red 473 yards.

Hole 12 indicates this is the twelfth hole. Par 5 means a skilled player will require 5 strokes to sink his ball from the tee box. Index 6 means this is the sixth most difficult hole. Black 526 reveals that the distance from the black tee box to the middle of the green is 526 yards. Blue 505 means the hole is located 505 yards from the blue tee box and so forth. Some courses use their own color codes.

Below is a brief guideline on how you could play each type of hole:

Par 3 Hole

A Par 3 hole ranges from 100 to 250 yards.

This is a short hole. You can usually see the flag and the dangers surrounding the green from the tee

box. With a suitable club, you should be able to reach the green with one stroke.

When playing this hole:

- Know where the flag is located. Flags are color-coded. A red flag means the hole is at the front of the green or closer. A white flag means the hole is located at the center of the green. A blue flag means the hole is located at the back of the green.

- What is the worst scenario here? Water? Sand? Slope? It's always better to putt up rather than down a slope.

- Use the club that will allow you to hit the distance. If in doubt, choose a longer hitting club.

Par 4 Hole

A Par 4 hole ranges from 251 to 475 yards.

Your primary goal here is to keep your ball in play. Hitting the ball farther means you have a shorter second shot. Study the diagram at the tee box. Given the yardage, can you reach the green in regulation? From the diagram, you must chart your passage to the green.

When playing this hole:

- You don't always need a driver to tee-off. Choose a club that will land your ball on the fairway.

- If you can't reach the green in regulation, hit your next shot to a location where you can play your best approach shot. If you're better at playing the bunker than a pitch shot, hit your next shot into a bunker.

- If you can reach the green, take into account the roll of the ball. Aim at the place that gives you the greatest margin for error.

- Aim away from danger rather than going for the pin or flag when playing your approach shot.

Par 5 Hole

A Par 5 hole ranges from 476 yards to 690 yards.

This is the longest and most interesting hole. For the professional, this is considered a scoring hole. This is where they can score a birdie or an eagle. For the beginner or high-handicap golfer, this can be a scary hole. Longer distance means more required strokes. And more strokes mean more mistakes!

Examine the diagram and plot your strategy. For a beginner, getting the ball on the green in 4 strokes is quite an achievement.

When playing this hole:

- Use your driver or a 3-wood to hit your ball farther.

- Because of the length of this fairway, you may encounter fairway hazards. Play to avoid them.

- Use the same last three shots strategy as a Par 4 hole.

You'll encounter these holes on a golf course. If you play the course repeatedly, you'll know the terrain well. You'll learn where to attack and where to avoid.

Besides knowing the terrain, you should take into account the weather. Playing after rain or in the wind differs. Morning play also differs from afternoon play.

Hey, we never said golf is an easy game!

GOLF INSURANCE

In the UK alone, more than 10,000 golfers a year incur injuries that require hospital treatment. Many injuries occur to another player, not to yourself. In April 1998, a court of appeal upheld a ruling that "golfers are liable for shots that cause injury, no matter how slight the risk".

Golf can be a very expensive game. The more you play, the more likelihood you will one day hit someone with your golf ball. In Great Britain, courts now rule that players are liable for an accident even if they shout "fore!" This happened after a Southampton golfer was ordered to pay considerable damages to another golfer who was hit in the eye by his accidental deflected shot.

Therefore, shouting "Fore!" isn't a guarantee of immunity for being sued. The best option is to purchase insurance. Ordinary household insurance won't cover accidents on the golf course. You must obtain golf insurance. Golf insurance will offer you financial protection and allow you to play a peaceful round.

Your equipment will also be covered for damage, theft or accidental loss. How many times have you left your pitching wedge on the green?

When obtaining insurance, make sure to discuss all aspects of the policy with your agent. Be sure he explains all the small print. Some insurance companies even offer a reward for a hole-in-one!

Don't be afraid to ask questions.

- Are you insured for courses overseas?

- Are you insured for playing other sports?

- Will your golf insurance cover you if you're injured on the tennis court?

- Is your equipment insured elsewhere?

GOLF HOW TO'S

How to Mark A Scorecard

All golf courses provide scorecards so you can keep track of each player's score. Players count all the strokes they use after completing each hole of the course. Then they write down the total in the corresponding box on the scorecard.

Although they may look a little different, all scorecards contain common information.

They all have a line called a "Hole" row, which corresponds to each hole of the course. They will also contain rows that indicate which tees are played and the yardages of each hole. The colors used for these rows varies according to the course.

The following scorecard also includes the layout of each hole at the top:

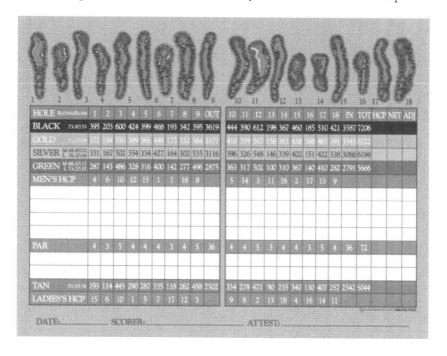

Course Handicaps

You may also notice rows with corresponding numbers showing Men's or Ladies Handicaps. They're used to help beginners even the playing field on the course.

Consult the chart to determine where you can reduce your score by one or more points or "take a stroke". Depending on your course handicap, you may end up taking strokes on several holes.

If you have a handicap of 5, you need to take a stroke form each of the five highest-rated holes on the scorecard. Bear in mind that 1 is considered the highest and 18 is the lowest.

If you are a real beginner, you may end up with a handicap of 18. This means you get to take a point from every hole of the entire course!

You should mark the holes where you use a handicap with a small dot. You should also use a forward slash to divide the corresponding boxes for these holes. Your actual number of strokes gets entered on the top and your net score (your actual score minus your course handicap) gets entered below.

Common Statistics

Players may also choose to record statistics on the scorecard. Some of the more common statistics include:

- **Fairways Hit** – This means your ball reaches the fairway with a tee shot.

- **Putts Taken** – This refers to the number of putts you use for each hole.

- **Greens In Regulation (GIR)** – This indicates whether your ball reaches the putting surface in 1 shot for a Par 3, 2 shots for a Par 4 or 3 shots for a Par 5 hole.

Circles & Squares

You may see scorecards with circles or squares surrounding some of the stroke totals. The circles represent holes that are below par, squares represent above par holes and the remaining numbers equal par holes. Some totals may be surrounded by two circles or squares. Here is the meaning of the symbols:

> ➤ **One Circle**   = **Birdie**

> ➤ **Two Circles**   = **Eagle**

> ➤ **One Square**   = **Bogey**

> ➤ **Two Squares**   = **Double Bogey**

We included this information so you'll understand the symbols if you see them.

However, beginners shouldn't worry about this system. There's no point filling up a scorecard with squares until you gain more practice!

How to Use a Ball Washer

Almost every course has a device called a ball washer. In fact, some courses provide one at every single hole! The ball washer was invented in 1934 and as the name implies, it's used to clean your golf balls during a game.

Although each ball washer may look slightly different, they all contain essential parts. They all include a round handle near the top and a long plastic body made containing water. Some ball washers may contain a detergent solution. Inside the body, strong bristles scrub away dirt and debris from your ball. A trash can or towel may be attached to some machines.

Why Use One?

Ball washers are very important because clean balls offer a better shot. A clean ball will travel farther and offer better backspin. It's easier to make clean contact with a clubface when using a clean ball.

Because golf balls have a rough surface, they tend to collect a lot of debris. Dirt, sand or parts of the turf interfere with the special aerodynamics of a golf ball and affect its trajectory.

This debris can transfer to the grooves or face of your club.

Method Used

1. Locate the nearest ball washer on the course

2. Grab the ball on top of the handle and pull straight up

3. You will notice a curved arm containing a hole where you place your ball

4. Move the arm up and down several times. Each time you do this, the bristles inside the machine will clean your ball.

5. Once you're finished, tap one side of the ball until it falls out at the top.

6. If a towel is attached, use it to dry your ball or use your own towel.

You are now ready to return to the course and hit that perfect shot!

How to Repair a Divot

Have you ever taken a big swing and then watched as a piece of turf went flying through the air right after your ball?

This is a very common occurrence in golf. After taking a good swing, you will likely produce what is called a "divot" on the fairway. A divot is defined as "a piece of turn torn up by a golf club in striking a ball". A golf ball can also leave a mark upon contact with the putting surface and is sometimes referred to as a "pitch mark".

Divots are a normal part of golf and are only considered problems if they aren't repaired correctly. Proper golf etiquette requires that you repair any damage that you do to the course during your game.

Why Should You Repair a Divot?

One reason is that leaving a divot will create an uneven playing surface which is unfair for the other players. An important example of this occurred in the final round of the 1998 US Open. Payne Stewart hit a perfect tee shot straight down the fairway. Unfortunately, when he approached his ball, he discovered that it had landed in an unrepaired divot mark!

Another reason to repair divots is because the grass in that specific area may die if the damage isn't fixed quickly enough. In fact, the grass may take 2-3 times longer to grow back in areas of the course that haven't been properly repaired.

Methods Used

Basically, there are 2 methods to repair divots:

1. Fill a divot with sand or a mixture of seed and sand. Make sure to fill the damaged area completely and then pat the sand down with your foot to smooth the area.

2. Find the piece of turf or sod that was removed and try to put it back in place. Hopefully you created a "clean" divot which means the turf was removed in one piece. If not, find as many of the pieces as possible and attempt to replace them as best you can. Then pat the area gently with your foot to smooth the surface.

You may be wondering how to determine which method to use.

The answer is very simple.

If a course wants you to use sand or a sand and seed mixture, they will provide it for you. They will attach a container that looks like a large cup holder to the golf cart. The container is usually attached to the frame of the cart.

If you don't see a container of sand, the course wants you to repair divots by replacing the turf manually.

Using a Divot Repair Tool

You can also use a two-pronged device called a "divot repair tool". When used properly, this tool will help you repair the damage you have caused to a course.

Method

1. Locate the mark left by your ball

2. Insert the divot repair tool into the outer edge of the divot, angled at approximately 45 degrees

3. Gently work the turf up and push it forward back into place

4. Repeat around the entire mark until the area is restored

Note: Don't inset the divot tool directly underneath the area or you'll expose the soil and damage the root system. Also be sure not to insert the tool and twist it or you will break off even more of the turf.

If you have enough time, don't be afraid to repair someone else's divot in addition to your own. You can do your part to ensure a positive experience for the other players.

Your fellow golfers and the course green keepers will appreciate your help.

How to Rake Sand Bunkers

Sand bunkers or sand traps are found on nearly every golf course to make the game more challenging. The picture below shows 2 sand bunkers – one on the lower left and another on the upper right.

All sand traps will contain a device called a rake. This object looks very much like an ordinary garden rake.

Proper golf etiquette requires you to rake the sand with this object if your ball lands in a sand bunker. This process is actually very easy once you learn how to do it properly.

- Locate the lowest spot of the bunker that is close to where your ball landed. This will become your entry and exit point.

Walking down a steep part of the bunker will cause erosion and damage the turf and stepping off a higher edge of the rim will leave deeper footprints by.

You also need to remember that the farther distance you walk, the more area of sand you will need to rake!

- Once you find the lowest point, enter the bunker with your rake. Contrary to popular belief, this action is permitted on any course. Just don't use the rake to test the sand conditions or improve your lie. These actions are against the rules and will cost you a penalty stroke.

- After you play your shot, use the rake to sweep the area where your club contacted the sand and your footprints. Pull the rake towards you as you move backwards towards the rim of the bunker. Make sure not to pull too much sand. Just rake enough so that the surface of the sand is even and no divot marks or footprints are visible.

- Once you have finished raking, exit the bunker and rake the area a few more times.

Where to Leave the Rake

At this point, you may wonder where you should leave the rake.

It's important to place the rake where it has the least chance of affecting another player's ball.

The rules whether you should place the rake outside or inside the bunker depend on the particular course. Most courses will reveal the rules on their scorecard or posted on bulletin boards inside their clubhouse.

If you're in doubt, always leave the rake outside of the bunker.

As noted by the USGA: "There is not a perfect answer for the position of rakes, but on balance it is felt there is less likelihood of an advantage or disadvantage to the player if rakes are placed outside of bunkers."

The main thing is to leave the sand bunkers in the same good condition you found them!

How to Clean Your Golf Clubs

Cleaning Your Irons

It's very important to clean your golf clubs, especially if you play often. Cleaning your clubs will prolong their life and allow you to strike the ball more effectively. Grass, dirt and mud that cling to the clubs can interfere with your shots.

One option is to purchase a special golf club cleaning kit. These kits are usually sold in most pro golf shops.

However, there is a very easy and less expensive method. You will only require the following basic equipment:

- Plastic bucket (if you don't use a sink)

- Mild dishwashing detergent

- Brush with soft plastic bristles (an old toothbrush works great)

- Old towel for drying

Method:

1. Add a little detergent to the bucket

2. Fill with warm water until suds form. Don't use very hot water as it can damage the clubs

3. Take clubs outside if you have access to a hose or place them in a tub or sink

4. Place the irons in the bucket until the heads are completely covered with water

5. Soak clubs for a few minutes. This loosens the dirt in the grooves of the clubface and breaks down the oils and course chemicals on the clubheads

6. Remove each club separately and scrub it with a brush. This cleans any dirt, grass and other debris from the clubface and is the most important step of the entire process.

7. Drag the brush across the sole of the iron and the back of the clubhead

8. To remove any dirt that has hardened over time, soak the irons for a longer period or use a stiffer brush. Never use a brush with wire bristles as it may damage the clubs.

9. Rinse each clubhead off with a hose or tap. Try not to splash water on the shaft of the clubs

10. Take a look to make sure all dirt is removed. If not, repeat the process

11. Use an old towel to dry the clubheads

12. Drag the towel up the shaft of the clubs to remove loose dirt

   Note: Never place clubs back in your bag while they are still wet

Cleaning Your Woods

The process for cleaning your woods is a little different from cleaning your irons. You should never submerge any woods made of persimmon or metal woods because this can ruin their finish.

- Quickly dip them into sudsy water or rub them with a moist cloth

- Dry them with a cloth or towel

- Use a brush with soft bristles to clean out the grooves on each wood

How to Clean Your Golf Club Grips

The grip is one of the most important parts of your golf club. Basically, the grip is what connects you to your club. The grip is where your hands make contact with the club and allows you to control all of your shots.

Over time, grime and dirt build up on the grips. The oil from your hands and chemicals from the golf course can add to the problem. Unfortunately, many golfers neglect grips completely. They don't realize that cleaning your grips will prolong their life and give you a better feel when you're taking a shot.

The good news is there are several ways to easily clean the grips. You can go to a pro shop where they can clean your grips for a fee. However, you can complete this task yourself with relatively little effort or expense.

You can wipe them with a moist cloth and then dry them with another cloth. You can also spray on a mild cleanser such as Windex and then wipe it off.

The following method takes a little longer, but is more effective at removing the buildup of dirt and grime:

- Fill your sink with warm water and add enough dish detergent to form lots of suds. Don't use really hot water as they may damage the grips.

- Use a wet cloth to grab the suds and rub them into the grip of each club.

- Rinse each grip under running water to remove all of the detergent. Try not to get any water on the shafts during the process.

- As soon as they're rinsed, dry each grip off with a dry cloth or towel. Dry the shaft if they are wet.

You should clean your grips on a regular basis to make them last longer and perform better.

Eventually your grips will need to be replaced. With age and exposure to the elements, the material will crack and your grips will harden and start to come loose.

This will affect your game negatively. More importantly, loose grips can injure another player if they come completely loose or cause you to lose control of your club after a swing. Experts advise that you change your grips every season if you play more than 20 rounds.

50 BEGINNER GOLF TIPS

There is always something new to learn in the strategic game of golf. Even professionals continue to perfect their shots and learn more about the game.

However, beginners need to learn the basics before progressing to more advanced shots. We're going to provide you with a wide range of beginner golf tips that will help you improve your game and reduce your frustration level.

Keep these tips in mind, the next time you're on the course or at the driving range. You are sure to improve both your swing and your score!

Tip 1: Putting Games

As a beginner, you probably need to improve your short putts. If so, try putting to a dime. This exercise will improve your focus and concentration. Here is another great putting drill: try sinking five balls in a row starting one foot away, and then increasing to two feet, three feet and so on. Continue until you miss a shot at which point you have to start all over again! Don't increase your distance until you have sunk all 5 balls in a row. You can practice these drills while waiting to tee off.

Tip 2: Pull The Rope!

If you have a slice problem, you most likely cut across the ball during your downswing. You need to learn the correct path for the clubhead. An easy way to accomplish this is to picture a rope attached to an overhead tree. At the top of your backswing, imagine pulling the rope straight down. This will bring your right elbow close to your side and provides your stroke the correct inside path. It will also enable you to swing out towards the target instead of across the ball.

Tip 3: Hold Up the Ball

You may be collapsing your left knee toward the right during your backswing. This action forces your shoulders to drop and your hips to sway and overturn. To correct this problem, picture your left knee moving out toward the target during the backswing. You should feel tension and stability in both knees. If this doesn't feel right, try imagining you're holding a basketball between your knees. This should do the trick!

Tip 4: Be a Hitchhiker

During your backswing, visualize placing your right hand in the hitchhiker position. When the club is at waist height, you should be able to look back and see your thumb pointing to the sky. You can also picture your hand in a handshake position with your palm facing neither up nor down. These visualizations will you correct the beginning of your swing!

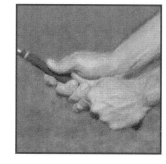

Tip 5: Pause at the Top

Many beginners tend to swing too quickly. Although you do need to swing with power and acceleration, you also need to maintain a rhythm. Take a slight pause at the top of your backswing before you change direction and begin your downswing. Try this and you'll discover that your ball will land in the middle of the fairway more often!

Tip 6: Eye on a Dime

Having trouble putting? Try this simple drill. Place the ball on top of a dime and focus your eyes on the dime throughout your stroke. Avoid the temptation to follow the ball with your eyes as soon as you have hit the ball, especially for short putts. Just continue to focus on the dime, rather than following the ball with your eyes, head and shoulders.

Tip 7: See Yourself in the Clubface

You need to keep your clubface "open" if you want to get out of the greenside bunkers. Closing the face results in a lower trajectory and causes your club to dig in the sand. Try this trick: Image that your clubface is a mirror and you will see your reflection in it at the end of your sand shot. This ensures you take your club all the way to eye level and that you keep it open all the way to the finish.

Tip 8: Check Your V's!

Many factors contribute to a slice. The most common is your grip. Here's a method you can use to fix this problem: When you are looking down during your address, make sure you can see the first 2 knuckles of your left hand and a "V" formed between your thumb and forefinger pointing toward your right shoulder. With your right hand, have the "V" pointing toward your chin or slightly to your right shoulder.

Tip 9: Bulls eye!

Three-foot putts can be a problem if you let them. Why not follow the strategy used by Seve Ballesteros, one of the all time great putters. Imagine a bulls eye attached to the back of the cup. This encourages you to accelerate the putter through and keep the clubface moving square to the hole!

Tip 10: Shoulder Under Chin – You Won't Hit It Thin!

Do you have a problem topping the ball or "hitting it thin"? If so, get in the habit of placing your right shoulder under your chin before looking to see where the ball lands. Don't keep your head down forever. You can let your head move, but allow your shoulder to bring it up after contact. If you do this correctly, you'll see the club hit the ball almost every time!

Tip 11: Step on It!

Practice proper weight shift by stepping with your right foot over your left after you hit the ball. You should feel as if you're walking to the right after contact. After each swing, ask yourself where the weight is. On your right or on left foot? A proper, balanced position should be 90% on your left foot and 10% on your right toe. Your momentum will naturally carry you to the walking position with right over left.

Tip 12: Hit Far With the Ball Forward

Depending on the club you're using, your position over the ball will vary. For example, the ball should be in the middle of your stand when using shorter irons such as 7, 8, 9 or PW. As the left of the club decreases, the ball should be incrementally farther towards your front foot until it is just inside your left heel when hitting the woods. If you want to hit a lower shot, remember that the ball should be back in the stance. The ball should be forward for higher shots.

Tip 13: Rock-Solid Right Knee

During your backswing, you have to keep your weight on the inside of your right foot and maintain a slight bend in your knee. If you don't, you end up with poor contact and a loss of power. As you take your club back, imagine that your right knee is braced and solid as a wall. This will help your upper body coil behind the ball so you can make an aggressive move through it and send it soaring!

Tip 14: Grip It Light On the Right

Normally your right side needs to remain solid for a strong shot, but not your grip. Many golfers grip their club too tightly with their right hand which leads to extra tension. This can also make you swing "over the top" and cut across the ball. Try this fix: Check your right side grip, arm and shoulder tension before you swing. You should sense a muscle tension corresponding to a 6-7 on a scale of 1 to 10. Light muscles are always better than tight muscles!

Tip 15: Muscle It!

Remember that golf isn't just a wrist game. You need to use the big muscles in your legs and trunk to achieve a powerful swing. Many beginners tend to hit the ball using only their arms and wrists. You may connect once in a while using this method. However, you need use your entire body, not just part of it for real consistency and power. Learn to muscle it!

Tip 16: Go Cross hand

A very common putting error involves a breakdown of the wrists. Try using a cross hand grip. Place your left hand down the grip where you right hand would normally be and then place your right hand on top of the grip. This may feel strange at first, but it will force your hands to work together as one unit. This is one of the fundamentals of good putting. Remember to always keep your hands in front of the ball and your left wrist flat during your stroke!

Tip 17: Splash Some Sand

The next time you find yourself in a bunker, focus on sliding a thin "divot" of sand from under the ball and on to the green. Open your clubface a few degrees clockwise and line up slightly to your left. Then splash the sand towards your target and your ball will follow!

Tip 18: Putt with Your Eyes Closed!

Have you ever tried to play golf with your eyes closed? You may be surprised at the answer. If you practice putting with your eyes shut, you will find it easier to feel your body movements. You should feel your shoulders working like a pendulum. The next thing you know, you will hear the ball hitting the bottom of that cup!

Tip 19: Hit Low Into the Wind

Many players tend to hit harder into a breeze. This actually causes them to put more spin on the ball and hit it higher. To hit a lower, more controlled shot, put the ball back in your stance a few inches and keep our hands forward. Use

a longer club than normal and swing easy. If you have trouble, remember this saying "Swing with ease into the breeze".

Tip 20: Wiggle Your Toes

Many golfers tend to move farther from the ball at address over time. Make sure you don't reach for the ball or place too much weight on the balls of your feet. Here is a test you can try: wiggle your toes at address. This may sound funny, but it will ensure that you don't place too much weight on the forward part of your foot!

Tip 21: Don't Choke It To Death!

Beginning golfers may assume they have to grip the club hard to hit hard. Actually, the opposite is true. A tense muscle is a slow muscle. Clubhead speed is essential for distance and light muscles always work faster. Try to attain a grip pressure of 5-6 on a scale of 1 to 10. Remember to grip your club lightly to hit the ball far!

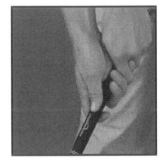

Tip 22: Weight Distribution Is Vital When Chipping

Proper weight distribution is essential to consistently getting the ball up and down. At least 60% of your weight should remain on your front foot at address or your left foot if you are a right-handed golfer. Picture hitting slightly down and through the ball. This encourages a proper transfer of weight and will help you complete the follow-through. Keep the back of your left wrist facing the target. If you let your wrist break down, your shows will break down as well!

Tip 23: Use Club Loft to Your Advantage

Make sure to hit down and through the ball if you want to send it airborne. If you let your club's loft to do the work, you'll achieve good contact and a natural flight path. Golf clubs have loft for a reason so always use it to your advantage!

Tip 24: Keep Your Head Still

Keeping your head still is essential for solid contact and consistent putting. Focus on not moving your head well after impact. Head movement causes your shoulders to open and your putter to cut across the ball. You can also try putting with your eyes closed. You may be surprised at the positive results!

Tip 25: The Toe Is Your Best Friend

Downhill putts are often fast and difficult. Therefore, why not take a tip from the experts: Hit the ball on the toe of your putter, not on the

sweet spot. This reduces the jump on the ball and prevents it from traveling past the hole. Remember, not to do this on uphill putts!

Tip 26: Bowl Your Way to Better Putting

You may be experiencing difficulty with putting distance control. If so, try standing in golf like address position and rehearsing several strokes without your putter. Then take a ball in your hand and roll the ball toward the hole. Once you feel comfortable determining how hard to roll the ball, pick up your putter and use the same motion to hit the ball!

Tip 27: Putt to the Pro Side of the Cup

Watch a pro when they are lining up a breaking putt. You'll notice how they always favor the "high" side of the hole, rather than the "low" side. The law of averages indicates that that gravity will work in your favor if the ball is above the hole as your putt is breaking near it. If your ball is breaking away on the low side, gravity will work against you. Just remember the pro side, not the low side and you'll sink more putts!

Tip 28: Swing Easy when it's Breezy

When you're playing in the wind, remember this simple, but effective saying "swing with ease into the breeze". This will prevent you from over swinging in the wind and your ball from sailing too high. Greg Norman used this tip during his 1994

British Open win!

Tip 29: Solidify Your Swing's Foundation

A smooth tempo and proper balance is necessary for a consistent golf swing. Just as a house requires a solid foundation, so does your golf swing does. Practice hitting several shots with your feet approximately 6 inches apart. This improves your balance, tempo and rhythm and is very effective when you return to your normal stance when hitting.

Tip 30: Turn Your Way to More Distance

When hitting a golf ball a long distance, you need to minimize your hip turn and maximize your shoulder turn. The easiest way is to keep your right knee firm and flexed throughout, and ensure that your left knee doesn't slide to the right during your backswing. Use the opposite knee if you are left-handed. You also need to get your shoulder behind the ball at the top of your backswing. This will ensure a proper weight shift and permit a longer swing.

Tip 31: Release Is the Key to Distance

The key to improving distance is a proper hand release during your swing. Take a short backswing and stop as soon as your club and hands are at waist level. Look as if you're shaking hands with your thumb pointing to the sky. As you swing down into the follow-through, ensure your hands are in the same position as your backswing (thumb facing up). This technique forces you to use your hands properly.

Tip 32: Swing through the Ball, Not At It

Most consistent, powerful swings have one thing in common – extension through the ball after hitting it. You can perfect this b placing a tee approximately 8 inches in front of the ball you're hitting. Try to hit not only the ball, but also the tee. This will train you to swing through the ball, rather than at it.

Tip 33: Make a Smooth Transition

Many amateur golfers ruin their opportunity to make solid contact by starting their downswing with a tense, violent motion. The top of the swing is a critical transition point and should lead quietly into a smooth downswing. An effective strategy is to think "light and lazy" at the top of your swing.

Tip 34: Remember, It's Just a Game

It's very important to remember that everyone plays golf to have fun. Too often, players become overly anxious about their performance. You can still try hard and concentrate on your swing. Just don't let the pursuit of perfection ruin your enjoyment of the game. Performance anxiety can interfere with the freedom of your swing and your spirit. Golf is just a game. Adopt this attitude at your very first tee and your performance and comfort level will rise!

Tip 35: Avoid Over Analysis Paralysis

These tips won't help if you become overly tense or analytical. Having a strong desire to improve is great, but you have to learn to relax. After a practice session or a game, hit a percentage of your shots with only the target in mind. This involves watching where you want the ball to travel, thinking positively and letting it go. Just grip the club and swing away!

Tip 36: Take It Back Low & Slow

Amateurs often take the club back too quickly with their wrists. This reduces proper tension and causes their swing to go off plane. Here's an effective drill to help you gain the proper feel for the take-away. Get into your normal address position and then place a ball behind your clubhead. As you start your backswing, roll the ball backward. Continue rolling the ball until it's well past your right foot. You'll feel your opposite shoulder move beneath your chin.

You'll realize how straight your left arm should be during your backswing.

Tip 37: Pass the Pole for More Distance

You need to use a proper weight shift to achieve maximum distance and consistency. Imagine a pole arising vertically from the ground where the ball is resting during address. During your take-away, concentrate on getting your left shoulder behind the ball and the imaginary pole without swaying your hips. This ensures a proper position to initiate your downswing. During your follow-through, move your right shoulder past the ball and imaginary pole. When performed correctly, you will make a good turn and proper weight shift.

Tip 38: Improve Your Balance & Game

If find it difficult to make good contact, you're most likely starting to sway, losing your balance or not turning. The following drill will help: Start by using short swings to hit shots with your feet approximately 6 inches apart. This exercise promotes proper footwork, balance and a free swing with your arms. It will also force you to turn more - you'll fall over if you don't! Once you feel comfortable making good contact, you can increase the length of your swings.

Tip 39: Make a Steep Swing in the Sand

This exercise will help you learn to take the club back in a more upright plane out of a bunker. By taking your club back more abruptly, you increase your chances of getting under the ball properly and impacting the sand more precisely. Have someone stand behind you in the sand and hold a rake approximately 2 feet behind your ball at a 45° angle. The goal is to swing up the rake handle as if your plane is steeper than your normal swing. Take several swings using this method and you'll find yourself hitting high, soft shots from the bunker!

Tip 40: Remember the Practice Area

The first place a pro golfer visits before heading to the first tee in a tournament is the practice area. You should also get in the habit of following this routine. Remember, you can warm up and loosen your muscles there, rather than worrying about how you're striking the ball. Once you're ready to hit, start with a wedge and then work your way down the set until you reach the driver. Finish with a few wedges. This promotes a proper tempo and feel which are vital to striking the ball correctly and can also prevent injuries!

Tip 41: Learn To Stay Flexible

Loss of flexibility and a resulting poor turn (like the one in the photo) is a very common complaint. The hip blocker is a very effective drill. When you fix your knees, your upper body is forced to turn more correctly and slowly increase flexibility. As you swing, remember to turn your shoulders as far back as possible until your left shoulder is under your chin. You will feel a greater stretch along your left side. Finish by repeating this on your follow-through, but

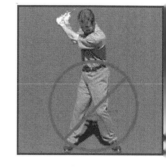

with your right shoulder under your chin. You'll eventually increase your ability to coil fully without using your hips. Remember, the power in your swing comes from a big shoulder turn and a minimal hip turn.

Tip 42: Increase Your Forearm Strength

Golf success requires left wrist and forearm strength. Many golfers break down their left wrist with their right arm dominating through impact. This causes many problems such as topping, loss of distance and shots pulling to the left. An effective strengthening drill involves holding the club straight out in front of you using the last 3 fingers of your left hand. Use your wrists to move the club up and down 10-12 times. Three slow, controlled sets without bending your arm will set the proper motion into your muscle memory.

Tip 43: Start at the Top

The secret to hitting a straighter, more consistent shot is to maintain a square clubface at impact. If your clubface connects squarely with the ball, your shots will fly straight. One way to promote this is by maintaining a square clubface at the top of your backswing. If your club isn't square, you need to manipulate it on impact which causes many timing problems. This drill is effective for teaching you how to play from a square position. With a club in your hand, lift your arms up to

your forehead and rotate your shoulders as far as possible, allowing a full backswing. This places your hands in a square position at the top and encourages a complete turn. Try to hold this position for a few seconds so you get the proper feeling at the top of the swing.

Tip 44: Act like a Baseball Player

A controlled, but aggressive weight shift is required for a proper golf swing. However, many players get stuck on their right foot and don't completely shift which causes poor shots. Try teeing a ball and adopting your normal address position. Then bring your left foot back so your feet are approximately 6 inches apart. Take a normal backswing, but just as begin down, step forward as if you were a home run hitter stepping on to the pitch. You may need to down your swing to hit the ball solidly. This will give you an accurate feeling of shifting and train you repeat the motion.

Tip 45: Stabilize Your Left Knee

Longer hitters display a significant inconsistency between hip and shoulder turn. A big hip turn is required during your follow-through, not your backswing! Your left knee is an important body part that affects what your hips do. When it collapses or bends inward, your hips turn too much which makes it impossible to create the necessary torque to build clubhead speed. An

easy solution is to feel your left knee remaining outward toward the target at the top of your backswing. This maintains distance between your knees.

Tip 46: Turn & Burn

There's an easy way to give you the feeling of a proper shoulder turn without your hips getting too involved. Sit on the edge of a golf cart and put a club on the line of your shoulders to simulate address. Then turn back and try to get the shaft pointing straight in front of you. You'll feel a lot of stretch on your left side which is good. This will help you get behind the ball more efficiently and will result in a few extra yards.

Tip 47: Dirty Those Shoes

You can tell a lot about golfers by looking at their shoes. If their shoes are older and their right toe is completely clean, there's a problem. When you shift your weight properly, you end up balanced on your right toe. This action eventually wears down that toe. Try to get your right toe dirty and beat up! This indicates that you are shifting your weight properly.

Tip 48: Point Your Way

The direct action of your hands affects the position of your clubface and the flight of your ball. Take your grip and adopt a normal stance, but point your finger down the shaft so it's pointing at the ball at address. Check the club when it's parallel to the ground on both your backswing and follow-through. Your finger should point down the target line on the return and at the target on the way.

Tip 49: Use Both Sides

For many players, your right side dominates a weak left arm and side during downswing and through impact. This causes poor extension and other swing flaws. Swing lightly with your left arm only to maintain a proper feel. As you do this, check how your arm extends freely through the impact zone. Then add your right arm with a light grip and try to maintain the previous extended feeling. You'll feel it becoming more restricted right away. Just let it go and continue to use your left arm and side along with your right.

Tip 50: Swing inside the Barrel

Golfers often continue to widen their stance. This is good for stability, but it permits lateral movement which can develop into a sway. The barrel drill can correct this. Keeping your stance approximately shoulder width apart, imagine 2 straight lines coming out of the ground outside

your heels. This allows for some lateral movement, but a full turn is normally required to avoid hitting the lines. Visualize yourself swinging in the barrel and wait for the low scores to follow!

GOLF LESSONS

Now that you've had a chance to review our 50 Beginner Golf Tips, we're going to provide you with 25 lessons. These will help you improve your scores and deal with a wide variety of common techniques and problems.

These lessons are great for beginners like you who are just learning the game!

Lesson 1: *Six Habits That Will Help Your Handicap*

The simplest advice often pays the greatest dividends. That's been our experience for many years. Most golfers hope for a magic tip or want to be enlightened about the intricacies of grip, stance and posture. However, all they really need are some good golf habits!

So here is our list of the six top ways to lower your scores and your handicap:

1. Move Up

Having trouble achieving a mental breakthrough? Try playing from the forward tees to alter your comfort zone and lower your scores. Playing a shorter course will instill a "go-for-par" or birdie mindset that will stick with you when you return to your accustomed tees. If you can't score any better from the forward tees, consider it a message that you require extra work on your short game!

2. Do It Daily

Ben Hogan once said he hated to miss a day of practice because it meant one more day before he could get better. While you may not be able to keep this regimen, you should keep in mind that you get out what you put into the game. Pressed for time? Just taking a club out in the backyard and swinging for 15 minutes will help.

3. When You Play Golf, Play Golf

If you're going to take the time to play, do it seriously and focus on each shot. Never make a careless swing during a serious round! Of course, this doesn't mean you can't have fun. It just means you should turn up the focus. Use the driving range for working on technical skills and the golf course for focusing on the real target: lowering your score!

4. Purchase Better Gear

We're not saying you should spend thousands of dollars on equipment. But if you're using an older set that isn't fitted properly, you may be holding yourself back. Many recent technical advances such as perimeter weighting to produce a larger sweet spot and larger club head volumes will make a difference in the consistency and distance of your shots. Why not take advantage of them?

5. Don't Shortchange Your Short Game

Chipping and putting account for more than half the strokes in a typical golfer's game. Consequently, you should devote most of your practice to your short game. I like to use a football analogy: It's great to be able to advance to the two-yard line, but it won't mean a thing if you can't make it into the end zone!

6. Write It Down!

It's easier to improve if you can document your hits and misses. Where do you hit good shots, and where do you hit poor ones? Did you hit right, left, or on top? How many putts of less than five feet do you miss? Keep a journal and consult it periodically to unearth patterns and discover areas that need work.

Good luck and have fun!

Lesson 2: How to Develop the Perfect Pre-Shot Routine

Most skilled golfers have a pre-shot routine – rituals that include everything from the way they approach the ball to how they waggle.

These routines serve a good purpose. When you approach your shots the same way each time, you train your subconscious to be less affected by outside influences such as pressure, wind, spectators or jibes from your foursome. Fewer variables in the moments leading up to your swing will mean fewer variables during your swing.

How should you develop your personal pre-shot routine? Here are some guidelines:

1. Do What Works For You

Factors such as how you arrive at your grip and stance, look at the target, waggle the club and take practice swings are all personal preferences. The exact details are less important than performing the same action consistently. Many pros even time themselves from start to finish to get within seconds on each swing – you might want to do the same. A good routine won't take a lot of time. Quickly, but methodically, review the checklist, think positive and hit the ball. Your

ritual should give you a positive feeling about the shot. Once you've completed the routine, trust it, be target oriented and let it go. You don't want to start wondering about your grip or the depth of the water during your backswing!

2. Get Lined Up

Try this in practice: Lay a club on the ground next to the ball and aim it toward the target. Then take a look at the club from behind to ensure it's positioned correctly. Put another club parallel to it close to where your feet would be. For your shot to go straight, the "foot line" should face slightly left of the target. You should also ensure that your knees, hips and shoulders are aligned. Practice this a few times and then perform it without clubs on the ground. Alignment is one of the simplest mistakes to correct. Poor alignment is one of the most destructive, because you must compensate for it in your swing.

3. See It Happen

Skilled players talk about "feeling" a good shot before it occurs. You can develop this feeling by creating a positive image of the ball's flight before you hit it. This visualization prevents negative thoughts. Stand behind the ball and imagine it traveling straight toward the target before landing softly on the green. Or picture a great shot from the past just like the one you're about to make. For beginners, a realistic goal might be to "see" the ball getting up in the air. Studies have shown  that players tend to achieve the result they envision. The mind has enormous control over the body so use it to see what you want, not what you don't want! Be target-oriented rather than trouble-oriented.

4. Reflect On Your Successes

When you hit a good shot, soak it in! Watch the ball's flight and how it lands and rolls. Hold your finish and try to mentally reinforce what the swing felt like. Giving yourself this positive feedback will make it much easier to recall these images and feelings during your pre-shot routine. When poor shots occur (as they do for all of us), don't spend too much time thinking about them. Devote your mental energy to producing good shots!

Lesson 3: Five Steps to Develop the Perfect Putt

Putting is often called a game within a game because many of the skills you require to be a good putter differ from those required for the rest of the game. In fact, studies show that putting accounts for 43% of the shots among better players. You'd be hard-pressed to find a great golfer who isn't a skilled putter!

Given these facts, it makes sense for time-pressed golfers to focus on their putting. Ironically, most students ask for tips on everything but putting. If you're serious about lowering your scores, try following these five simple steps to putting perfection.

1. Position

Position yourself so your eyes are over the intended line of the putt (ball line). Hold your putter loosely and directly under your eyes as you address the putt and let gravity take it straight down. When you look down at your putter, make sure it covers the ball. If not, move forward or backward. Ball position should be slightly forward, toward the left foot. Hands should also be forward. Align the putter shaft with your left forearm. This position promotes a good roll as the ball leaves the putter face.

2. Grip

Your hands should work together as a unit, not spread apart. The farther apart your hands, the more likely you'll use your wrist which isn't desired. The putting stroke originates in the shoulders and arms. Use a normal grip, with 3 fingers of each hand on the club and the others just along for the ride. Use relatively light (5 on a scale of 1-10) grip pressure in order to promote feel.

3. Aim

Find a target and imagine a straight line through the center of your putter. Don't worry about the line your feet make, but ensure the putter face is square to the target. This is the line your stroke should follow. Don't tilt your head or you'll distort the perspective.

4. Stroke

Your putting stroke should be dominated by the shoulders and arms and involve as little wrist movement as possible. Minimize body movement and try not to shift weight or turn the hips. In other words, forget much of what you've learned about the body's role in a full swing!

5. Acceleration

Successful putters have a backswing and follow-through of equal length. This promotes acceleration and aids distance control. One of the most common faults involves players taking the club way back and then stopping at the ball on the down stroke, anticipating the hit. Remember to stroke through the ball, not at it!

Lesson 4: Mastering the Second Most Important Club in Your Bag

It's been said that the driver is the second most important club in your bag, next to your putter. A good drive sets the tone for the rest of the hole. Will you be scrambling just to get back on the fairway, hoping for pars and bogeys, or will you be aggressively aiming for the green and for birdies? By squeezing a few extra yards out of those drives, the subsequent iron shot will be that much easier, as will your chips, putts, and so on:

1. Body Coil

Tiger Woods, Fred Couples and other greats generate tremendous power by coiling the upper body with a big shoulder turn. The hips, however, don't turn nearly as much. This creates tension and torque, not unlike a rubber band being stretched before it's released. How do you accomplish this? Try to keep the right leg and knee solid as you take the club away and fully rotate your shoulders. On the downswing, unwind and rotate through the ball with your hips. Make  sure your navel is facing the target at the end of the swing to ensure a full turn.

2. Developing a "Lag"

Successful drivers all have a "lag" in their swing. On the downswing, the wrists must release their energy at some point. *When* this happens is the key. The closer to impact with the ball, the more stored power. Many golfers deliver this source of power near the top of the swing or early on the way down and end up swinging with just arms at contact. This is commonly called "casting"--the opposite of lag. One drill is to cock your wrists at the top of the backswing so that there's a right angle between your arm and club. Pull the club down in slow motion, while doing your best to retain this angle. Try to incorporate this into your full swings and remember to release those wrists through the ball!

3. Swinging With the Entire Body

Some of the **biggest muscles in your body** are the upper legs and trunk, and you should use them to put power in your swing. On the downswing, your legs should begin the drive and the trunk begins the turn. The bigger muscles have much less chance to twitch under pressure than smaller ones. This is why good swingers seem to move effortlessly—the small muscles are being led by the larger ones. We call this "swinging with the whole body." Try it!

4. Left Arm Straight At the Top

Make sure your left arm is kept relatively straight on the backswing to ensure a wide swing arc. Keep some distance between the hands at the top of the swing and your shoulders and head. This produces more club head speed without swinging any harder. Davis Love III and Vijay Singh are great examples of this. Watch them and internalize what you see!

Lesson 5: Four Tips for Playing Golf in a Gale

When the wind blows, some players' games get blown away with it. Don't let this happen to you. Practice the techniques and what the very best golfers do: Use these adverse conditions to your advantage and learn to love the wind!

1. Playing In a Crosswind

Crosswinds are the most difficult playing situation. These winds will magnify any spin on the ball, and greatly reduce distance. If you slice or hook the ball, a crosswind will magnify the effect. Therefore, it's important to use these winds to your advantage. If you want the ball to land softly, such as on a green, try to curve the shot into the crosswind. If you want more distance, or to have the ball roll when it lands, "ride" the wind by curving it in the same direction as the crosswind. In general: play the ball low.

2. The Knockdown Shot

The "knockdown" shot can be used in many situations, but is especially useful in the wind. The key points are to avoid swinging at full speed, and to keep your hands in front of the ball. This hand position should remain at address and through impact. Many knockdown shots finish with the forward swing low and only half completed, with the wrists not fully released and definitely not cupped as in a normal shot. The main goal is to keep the ball low and under control.

3. Playing In a Headwind

This is where the knockdown shot really comes in handy. Play the ball back in the stance toward the right foot. Select more club to decrease trajectory. It's important not to swing as hard as on a regular swing (about 80% of normal). Remember what Greg Norman said on his way to winning the 1996 British Open: "Swing with ease into the breeze." This helps in 2 ways: It keeps the ball from having as much spin, and it won't fly as high, where it's especially susceptible to wind.

4. Playing In a Tailwind

Playing with a tailwind is great for your ego. Use less club and count on the ball flying and rolling longer. The wind also makes your shots travel straighter, even when mishit. If distance and carry are the goal, play the ball forward in the stance and hit it higher. Playing the ball back in the stance, as in the other wind situations, will make it a little easier to control - but remember to plan for the longer roll.

The most important thing in any windy situation is to hit the ball solidly. A well-struck ball will be much less affected than a mishit shot with sidespin. Spins in the wind get exaggerated, so watch out!!

Lesson 6: Finding the Fairway

How often have you birdied or even been able to par a hole after finding trouble off the tee? Hitting the fairway consistently is vital to playing well. However, it's not an easy task, especially in a pressure situation such as a tournament. The following are a few ideas to help you drive your ball in the fairway more often:

1. Visualize the Shot

Creating a **positive visual image** is critical in any sport but it's even more important in golf - a very mental game. The next time you're in the tee box, stand behind the ball and pick a target. Be very specific about your target rather than just aiming out there somewhere. As you stand behind the ball, picture yourself addressing the ball with the proper posture and alignment. Now, focus on the desired ball flight. Picture the ball launching off the clubface - high in the air and heading right  toward the target. Think back to a positive drive from another day in the same situation. Finally, step into the address position and let it happen. Remember, "seeing" what you want gives you a much greater ratio of success.

2. Swing within Yourself

Many good drivers will tell you they have a "bread and butter" shot and an all-out shot. When the fairway is wide and the situation allows, it's fine to grip it and rip it. But when you really need to land in the fairway, rely on a swing you can trust. Use the swing that gives you the highest degree of accuracy. This swing is usually an 80% swing speed accompanied by good rhythm and tempo. In addition, reducing the hip turn on the backswing is helpful. Remember, the key to this type of shot is to get the ball on line and rolling.

Tiger Woods often used this tee shot during the U.S. and British Opens this year. When executed correctly, your ball will fly low, straight and roll a lot - down the fairway.

3. Stay Balanced

As we mentioned in other lessons, balance is critical in achieving consistent results with the driver and all other parts of the game. After you've swung, you should be able to stand tall with your body fully turned toward the target for a few seconds without losing your footing. If you're at all shaky, it's time for some practice. A good drill is to make a slow and complete practice swing. This slower motion will help to train your muscles. It also makes it easier to keep your balance. Eventually, you'll be able to increase your practice swing speed while retaining the balance at the end of the follow-through.

4. Use the Right Tools

This is the hard part and can take a while if you're just randomly trying clubs. This is where club fitting can really speed up the process of improving your game. No two golf swings are alike. The best club for you might be the worst for someone else. **Having the perfect fit is very important** in helping you find the fairway.

Lesson 7: Many Players are Afraid of the Right Side. Don't Be!

Students often tell me that they have "too much right-side emphasis" in their swings. They have usually been told this by well-meaning teachers.

In most instances, the right side is getting a bad rap. In reality, it's a golfer's biggest asset! Among right-handed players, it provides most of the power.

You really can't have too much right side in your swing, but you can use it improperly. To illustrate the power your right side possesses, try pushing as hard as you can against a fixed object such as a golf cart that is approximately 3 feet off the ground. Make sure your right elbow is close to your side in front of your right hip. Now try the same thing with your left arm pushing into the cart with the back of your wrist, as in a golf swing. No power there! The reason? The right hand is taking advantage of the full body: trunk, legs and torso. In contrast, the left arm is pulling away from the body, making it difficult to generate power. Like a boxer throwing a punch, you're using a full body rotation with your right side - not just the arm.

1. Drop at the Top

That gets golfers into trouble with the right side is often called "coming over the top." This means that the downswing is being initiated by the upper body, particularly the right shoulder and arm. To correct this, think of your hands and arms lightly dropping for a few inches from the top of the backswing. This puts the right elbow where it should be--close and connected to the right hip as you start to turn *see photo*. Don't try to keep the elbow close on the backswing, however, as this will create a very flat and narrow swing.

2. Get Your Train on Track

The other problem is when the right hand becomes overactive and dominates the left. This causes a breakdown of the left arm and a "cupping" of the wrists. Here's how to fix the problem: Think of the right as the locomotive, and the left as the train tracks. The left channels power down the proper path toward the target. To get a feel for this, swing with the left arm only. As you come through, ensure that the left shoulder turns naturally, and away from the chin. If this doesn't happen, you'll likely see lot s of shots go to the right.

Lesson 8: How to Turn Bunker Play into a Day at the Beach

Let's face it, everyone has to dig themselves out of the sand sooner or later. Fortunately, there are simple, reliable techniques for blasting out of bunkers. Good sand play doesn't just involve technique - equipment is also crucial. Therefore,

we have also covered the essential aspects of a good sand wedge.

Read on for everything you need to know so you enjoy your next day at the beach:

My Favorite Tips

- Use swing speed to alter distance. Practice until you can gauge distance by your personal swing speeds.

- Make the clubface enter behind the ball at a steep angle to hit shorter, and a shallower angle to hit longer. A steeper angle allows the club head to get under the ball and lift it.

- Take 2-3 inches of sand with each shot (see photo). Less sand will spin the ball more, but is risky. Practice by drawing a line in the sand behind the ball and hit that spot.

- Establish firm footing by digging the feet in slightly.

- Use an open stance (left foot spread to the left) to restrict backswing length and steepen the swing.

- Open the clubface slightly to offset the open stance. Open it more if you want a higher, softer shot.

- Keep your wrists firm through impact and don't release your hands until well after impact.

- Visualize a steep, "U-shaped" swing.

Beach Clubs

It's important to understand sand wedge design and how it can work for you. A **well-designed wedge** has three important characteristics:

- "Bounce" describes the rounded sole of the club head. Sand wedges have this to allow the club to glide, skid or bounce rather than dig into the sand.

117

- "Loft" or angle of the clubface is crucial for getting the ball in the air, over the edges of bunkers, and to ensure that it lands softly. Sand wedges generally have a loft of 56-60 degrees. By comparison, a pitching wedge is 48-52 degrees.

- "Toe-heel camber" is what gives sand wedges an oval-shaped look on the bottom of the face, to prevent the toe or heel from catching. Think of the club "splashing" through the sand rather than digging.

Remember, you're making things unnecessarily difficult if you're using a **pitching wedge** to get out of the sand!

Make It Happen In the Mind's Eye

Tension can ruin your sand shot faster than anything else. When tension occurs, the swing is inhibited and so is the chance for a good shot. Try to visualize a good shot. Stay muscularly light and mentally positive. Gary Player, one of the worlds' best bunker players, once remarked, "If I am one of the greats, it's for one simple reason: no bunker shot has ever scared me and none ever will. Approach every bunker shot with the feeling you are going to hole it."

Lesson 9: Our 6 Best Tips for Hitting From the Rough & Other Tough Lies

I don't care how good a golfer you are--at some point you'll be stuck in a bad lie. It happens to all of us! Getting the ball out of the rough can be quite a challenge--especially if you don't have a strategy. Here are some tips to help bail you out of a bad situation, and just maybe have some fun doing it!

1. Stand Closer At Address

Standing slightly closer to the ball will create a more upright swing plane, which means the club will encounter less grass on the downswing.

2. Open the Clubface

Opening the clubface clockwise at address helps in 2 ways: First, it gives the shot more loft which helps it get airborne. Second, the rough often grabs the clubface and pulls it left, so opening it helps keep the shot on line.

3. Move Your Stance Forward

When using the short irons, moving forward over the ball will promote a steeper swing and help "punch" the ball out without catching too much grass.

4. Adjust Your Distance

Rough tends to take backspin off the ball and create a "flier" that goes farther and takes longer to stop. Adjust your target to allow for the added roll.

5. Use a Steeper Approach

On the downswing, you should feel as though you are hitting "down and through" with a sharper swing. Don't be afraid to move some grass and take a divot. This is one time to be aggressive!

6. Adjust Your Grip

We normally recommend light grip pressure. However, when hitting in the rough, the left hand should be slightly tighter. By doing so, the club won't turn over when it hits the grass or pull the shot to the left.

Lesson 10: Our Best Tips for Hitting out Of a Sidehill Lie

In an ideal world, we wouldn't hit balls into embarrassing lies in the first place. But the fact is, we all do it, no matter how good or well-practiced a golfer we are. Consequently, it pays to know how to get out of these situations!

One of the most difficult is the side hill lie where the ball is above or below your feet.

Here are some tips that will improve your chances of a successful escape:

Ball above the Feet

In this situation, the most common mistake is hitting behind the ball and making it go too far left. To fix these problems you should:

1. Choke down on the club. The amount depends on the severity of the slope.

2. Aim to the right and open the clubface slightly (turn it clockwise). The ball tends to go left from this type of lie because the slope pulls it that way.

3. Reduce knee flex. It's less likely that you will hit the ball "fat" or behind this way.

Ball below the Feet

In this situation, the most common mistake is hitting the ball too far right and topping it. To fix these problems, you should:

1. Grip near the end of the shaft to help avoid hitting it "thin" or on top.

2. Aim slightly left. The ball tends to go right from this type of lie.

3. Use more knee flex. This helps avoid hitting the ball "thin" or on top.

Lesson 11: How to Be At Your Best in the Rain & the Cold

A strong mental attitude is critical when nature's forces are trying to knock you off your game. Try putting these countermeasures in place and you may just learn to love winter!

Rain

Keeping clubs and grips dry is critical when it starts to rain. Once grips get wet, your performance and desire will decrease dramatically. Professionals have caddies to take care of this. The rest of us need to take the time to place a cover or towel over the opening of the bag. If you have an umbrella, hang a couple of dry towels on the spokes. This way you'll always be able to dry off the grips and your hands, no matter how wet everything else gets. If you wear a glove, remove it after each shot and keep it in a dry place - under the umbrella is a good spot. Invest in some high-quality rain gear. Many of the new, high-tech fabrics really work, keeping you dry without causing you to sweat or get soaked from the inside out.

Also, remember that the ball won't travel as far in the rain, and the ground will be wet, decreasing roll. Many players fail to use **enough club** in wet conditions.

Cold

When the air is cold, the ball won't travel as far, so you should choose more club here as well. Good chipping and putting can make up for other mistakes in cold conditions, but you must have good feel; this means keeping your hands warm. When US pros play in icy weather at the Dunhill cup in Scotland, they're wear warm gloves between shots and place hand warmers in their pockets. Make sure you have a way to keep your hands warm before you tee off!

You should also choose a softer compression golf ball. This will help you keep a sense of feel around the greens and elsewhere.

Wind is also a major factor in winter. For tips on how to hit when it starts to blow, see our previous lesson on the topic. Remember to have fun out there!

Lesson 12: Our Five Best Tips to Help You Hit Woods with Confidence

You will be probably be playing a fairway wood on the second shot of a long par-5 hole. Woods can always out-distance irons because of their longer shaft length and bigger head. However, they're harder to use.

Because of their length, you can't approach a fairway wood the same way as an iron. Your swing plane needs to be shallower or more horizontal. You want to sweep the grass instead of making a divot.

Practice sweeping the grass until you can consistently hit the target. Then try to hit your target and sweep more grass. You should be able to sweep about 4 inches of grass. You should see blades of grass being flattened and a path being formed. As with all other swings, your hands and arms should be relaxed.

Now that you can consistently sweep the grass, you should be able to sweep the grass when there is a ball lying there. Hopefully, your mind won't be overloaded with the extra image. If you can disregard the presence of the ball and repeat your sweeping swing, you're on your way to mastering the fairway woods.

Like they say, "The ball just happens to be in the way."

Here are a few thoughts to take with you to the range:

1. Make a Full Turn

As your body ages, flexibility diminishes. Don't feel bad, it happens to everyone. So does your ability to make a full turn. If you're serious about improving, you must stay flexible. Fairway woods require a full turn of the torso and upper body without overturning the hips, to maximize distance. There are many good stretches you can do to slow down the aging process and increase flexibility! Try sitting down and resting a wood behind your neck with your hands holding the  club lightly above your shoulders. Now, slowly stretch and rotate from side-to-side, turning your shoulders as close to 90 degrees as possible in relation to your hips.

2. Take a Proper Stance

Longer clubs will change your swing plane, usually making it flatter as you stand farther away from the ball. So when hitting longer clubs, particularly woods, you must focus on several things. Make sure you retain good posture. At address, flex your knees and feel as though your behind is sticking out. A good drill is to have someone hold a club along your spine. Bend forward by tilting your pelvis, and keep your back flat, not arched. This also allows your hands and arms to fall naturally from the shoulders without reaching too much for the ball. Visualize keeping the spine perpendicular to the shaft at address.

3. Watch Your Ball Position

Normally your shorter irons are played from the middle area of the stance. With fairway woods, it's a different story. Move your stance so the ball is off of the left heel (right heel for left-handed players). This allows for a greater sweeping motion as you swing. Having the ball too far back in the stance will make your approach too steep and cause you to take a divot. If you make a deep divot with a wood, it's usually because your swing is too steep.

4. "Sweep" The Ball

The proper swing arc with woods is long, wide and smooth - contrary to a short iron's arc. When hitting woods, you should feel like you are sweeping the ball from the turf and extending through the ball. The backswing should also be deeper and the follow-through extended. This means the swing arc is wider. One of the best tips to encourage this movement is to imagine striking through a ball a few inches in front of the one you are hitting. Eventually, you'll learn to hit through it - not at it!

5. Do the Waggle

A low ball flight is often caused by a closed clubface. Although this gives your shot plenty of roll, it will also hamper your ability to get the ball airborne and affect distance control. This closed-clubface problem often starts with the takeaway. Practice the waggle drill in which you fan the clubface open during the first foot or two of the backswing. This puts your hands in a good position at the top of the swing and ensures a proper wrist cock.

Lesson 13: Know Your Faults & How to Fix Them

When you get the urge to get your game in shape, make a plan and stick to it. As with golf and anything else in life, a little planning goes a long way toward success.

Work On One Drill

If you're swaying, for instance, only work on that. A common mistake many of us make is that we lose our focus. If you hit a bad shot because you lifted your head too soon, don't change your practice thoughts. Remain focused on how to avoid swaying. Otherwise, you'll go around in circles, never accomplishing anything! Continue **working on one swing thought until you've perfected it.** Only then should you move on to another area such as lifting the head too soon.

Practice like You're Playing

If you're at the range hitting balls, don't smash them recklessly. Practice each shot with a purpose. Remember, your time on the range should be constructive. The more real you can make it, the more valuable it becomes when you're on the course. This doesn't mean you always have to be ultra-serious. Just approach each shot as though there is a goal. This creates muscle memory and is the way all good players approach practice!

Breakdown You're Game

It's important to break down your game before every practice session. Golf can be broken down into four main areas: ball striking, short game, **mental game** and course management.

How do you rate your game in each of these areas?

When you know, devote the majority of your practice time to the weaker areas. This will benefit you in the long run.

What follows is a list of points to work on when you're practicing golf's essentials:

1. **Ball Striking**: Most golfers spend their time working in this area. The fact is that ball striking tends to be a more important area for beginners than accomplished players. You should practice this - but not only this!

2. **Short Game:** The short game is comprised of chipping, pitching and putting. This is the one area where you'll be able to shave a few strokes, if you devote enough time to it. If you don't agree, just add up the strokes in an average round. Often, you'll find that more than half are spent here.

3. **Mental Game:** In no other sport is the mental game more important. In golf, it's just you against the course. Therefore, it's critical to learn how to deal with emotions and create positive images. Whether you're shooting your best score or your worst, emotions can affect any round. Anger can be beneficial if you channel it into positive action. Unfortunately, most people are affected negatively by it and lose concentration. How do you hold up under pressure? Find a way to approach each shot the same way. This will help you to become more consistent. This is the basis of sports psychology.

4. **Course Management:** Jack Nicklaus was never known for his ball-striking ability, but was able to win as a result of his golf course management. Playing smart means that you know the limitations of your game, and you are able to manage them. Play to your strengths not your weaknesses! Do you know when to go for a green and when to lay up? Understanding this facet of your game is important.

Practice A Pre-Shot Routine

The more consistent your routine before you hit a shot, the more steady your play will be. Take some time to develop a checklist or routine and keep it simple! In a short time, it will become habit - steering you toward better all-around golf.

Lesson 14: 5 Ways to 10 More Yards

How would you like to reach each par 5 on your home course in just two shots? What if you could **hit a 5-iron** instead of a 3-iron into a long par 4? Odds are that your game would improve. Here is a list of what I consider the five essentials to focus on if you want to hit the ball farther.

1. Widen Your Swing Arc

Tiger Woods and Davis Love are good models of long hitters with wide take-aways and big arcs. To achieve this, extend your arms as much as possible on the backswing. If you can keep your arc wide, you'll be able to create good clubhead speed without swinging any harder.

2. Lighten Your Grip Pressure

You don't have to swing hard to hit the ball a long way. In fact, this is often counterproductive and causes muscle tension. This will ultimately lead to less club head speed. After relaxing your upper body, the next key in attaining additional power is proper grip pressure. Think of your grip pressure as about a 7 on a scale of 1 to 10. Maintain this pressure throughout the swing to create good club head speed and still maintain control. If you have access to a club head speed analyzer, put your swing on it. While using the device, note the difference in your club head speed when applying tight- and relaxed-grip pressure. You'll quickly discover that the less tension you have in your body and grip pressure, the more your club head speed increases.

3. Make a Big Shoulder Turn

Jim McLean, one of the PGA's best teachers, calls shoulder turn the "X" factor. He took scientific measurements of many long hitters and found that they all have a greater shoulder than hip turn. This means that a big hip turn can actually diminish your ability to create power and club head speed because there is less torque created. Keep the lower body (the foundation) steady while the shoulder gets behind the ball, and you'll be in good shape.

4. Tuck Your Elbow

The best way to feel the proper position is to keep the right elbow tucked against your side on the downswing (left elbow for left-handed players). By doing this, you'll avoid the common error of swinging across the ball which diminishes power. Also, keeping the right elbow in delays the hit with your hands - essential in creating power and a properly timed release. When you perform the tuck correctly, the right arm (for right-handed players) is straight and your hands are not behind the ball.

5. Keep Your Knees Firm & Flexed

Think of your legs as the foundation of your swing. If your foundation is shaky and moves around too much, you'll suffer a power leak and lose ability to coil properly. Keep a firm feeling with the right knee at the top of the backswing (left knee for left-handed players) and a feeling of your weight staying on the inside of the foot. If the knee and weight move outside the foot, a sway can occur which causes numerous mechanical problems. The left knee should stay fairly still and not move laterally too much so that you maintain some width between the knees. One of our 50 beginner tips suggests that you imagine you're holding a basketball between your knees.

Lesson 15: Learning To Manage Your Game

After you've learned the fundamentals of the golf swing, the next challenge to improve your game involves proper course and game management. If you watch enough Tour events on television, you'll hear announcers talk about the importance of course and game management. All players on Tour hit the ball well and they all have solid, all-around games. Yet, only a certain percentage of them ever win. Until a Tour player learns to perfect the management of the game, the player seldom wins. For years, Jack Nicklaus was considered the best at this. Course management is best defined as playing smart golf. It's about understanding your game inside and out, your limitations, when to

gamble on a shot and when to back off. The two most important areas you can manage on the course are your judgment and emotions.

To play your best, try implementing the following strategies the next time you golf:

Develop a Routine

Indecision, doubt and hesitancy lead to poor golf swings. **Believe in yourself and play with confidence**! Learn to accept that you'll hit bad shots and swing without that fear and pressure. Ben Hogan *(above photo)* often claimed that 90% of hitting a golf ball occurs before the swing. Take a positive approach and visualize what you want rather than what you don't want. Approach each shot as an opportunity for a great result, rather than bringing bad past experiences and fear to the shot. You'll find that maintaining the same pre-shot routine and approach every time - both mentally and physically - will help you when you're angry, nervous or feeling other strong emotions.

Control Your Emotions

Some sports reward you for getting angry or emotionally pumped up and excited. In golf, such strong emotions can hurt you unless they're properly channeled. Try to stay even-keeled, using the same approach to each shot whether you've just birdied or triple bogied. It's fine to celebrate a great shot or be angry with a poor one for a few moments. But, by the time you address your next shot, you should have the same feeling you had on the first tee.

Choose the Right Club

Before you get up there and swing away, determine the correct distance to the hole. These days, most courses have yardage markers. Make sure you take advantage of them and pay close attention to detail. Is the yardage marker's distance measured to the front or center of the green, and where is the flag in relation to that distance? This can easily be a difference of two or three clubs. Firm course conditions also affect how far you should plan for the ball to carry. In time, paying close attention helps you determine how far, on average, your shots carry. Remember to factor in trouble. Determine if there is more trouble short of the green or over it, and favor more or less club accordingly. Doing this helps to minimize your score even when you mishit the ball. Furthermore, several other factors can influence your ball's flight and carry. Remember to take wind, rain, rough and your lie into account and adjust accordingly.

Take Advantage of Tee Boxes

The only time you can change your ball's placement is when you tee it up. Take advantage of this! Always favor the same side as the trouble to get the best angle and the best percentage for avoiding it. This way, you face away, rather than into the trouble.

Weigh the Risk & Reward

If you hit a poor shot, sometimes you have to accept your "medicine" and chip out of the rough and back to the fairway. Ask yourself, what could happen if you miss the shot you are attempting? If you hit those trees you are trying to slip the ball around, will it cost you just one shot or could the decision add several more to your scorecard?

Swing With Ease

Don't try too hard to get extra distance. Forcing your swing is counterproductive because it causes a loss of balance and control. This is a mistake most amateurs make when faced with a long or difficult shot. If you can stand tall with good balance after your swing, you've probably done a good job of swinging "within" yourself. If not, choose an extra club and tone it down so that your balance is solid.

Lesson 16: Learn Seven Drills to Putt Consistently

A one-foot putt is just as important as a 300-yard drive. It's also interesting to note that you can hit every green in regulation and not score well - if your putts aren't dropping. Putting is perhaps the most important ingredient to scoring well. On the PGA Tour, everyone hits the ball virtually the same, but the player who putts the best each week will win the tournament. Here is a list of drills to help you sink a few more putts and shave a few strokes off your score in the process:

Use the Flagstick

Most golfers have trouble keeping their putter on the proper line during the stroke. Try using a flagstick to help define the path of your putting stroke. Simply lay a flagstick flat on the putting surface and line it up with the hole. Now set the heel of your putter against the flagstick. This works as a guide when you stroke the putt. Next, pay close attention to the putter, and maintain smooth contact with the flag on both the forward and backstrokes. By doing this, you'll be able to see exactly where your stroke goes off line and correct it.

Start With a Roll

Putting a perfect, true roll on the ball starts with correct ball position. The mistake many players make is that they play the ball too far back in the stance. This causes a descending stroke and can make the ball bounce initially, rather than roll. To get the ball rolling smoothly, play the ball further up in the stance - off the inside of your front foot. You'll notice that the proper position is under the left eye (right eye for left-handed players).

Close an Eye

Lifting the head not only hurts the full swing, but the putting stroke as well. Close the left eye (right eye for left-handed players), take a few practice strokes, and then address the ball. Doing this makes it tough to see the hole - but it's not necessary. Just focus on the ball with only the right eye (left eye for left-handed players) until you see the putter contact it. This drill trains you to keep the head and body still during the stroke.

Force a Bigger Follow-Through

Under pressure, short putts cause tension in a golfer's stroke. To maintain a good stroke, accelerate through the putt. Oftentimes, the backstroke becomes too big, causing deceleration on the forward stroke. To cure this, place a second ball about 6 inches behind the ball you're going to hit. On the backstroke, try not to strike the second ball. By restricting the backstroke, you'll force a bigger, more accelerated follow-through.

Don't Break Your Wrists

Stick a tee into the end of your putter grip. As you take your stroke, make sure that the tee stays even or slightly ahead of the **putter head** throughout the stroke. If the head passes the tee, you've probably broken your wrists and opened the door to inconsistency. On long putts, this is more difficult to do as they can require some wrist break. Therefore, use this drill for shorter, mid-range putts.

Surround the Hole

Find a hole on the practice green that has some slope. Place several balls around the hole, approximately 2 feet away. Now go around the circle, concentrating on making each putt and noticing how each putt breaks a little differently depending on its position. Challenge yourself to make each putt before graduating to moving the balls to 3 feet away. If you miss one, start again. Remember, the more you see yourself knock in these practice four-footers, the stronger your confidence will be.

Putt to a Quarter

Place a quarter on the putting green and practice putting to it. By using a smaller target, you will refine your ability to aim for and locate the center of the cup. This is also a good drill for developing the feel of speed on longer putts.

Putting is extremely important to lowering your scores. The next time you work on your game, devote as much time to putting as you do hitting balls. You'll enjoy the results.

Golf course and game management entail developing consistent habits, being aware and using common sense. Give these tips a try and watch those scores come down!

Lesson 17: Our Six Ways to Eliminate Your Slice

Playing golf with a slice, an uncontrollable shot that curves left to right, is a problem many golfers think they have to live with and accept. This isn't true - even if you've been a chronic "slicer" for years. With a little time, dedication and effort, you can learn to stop hitting stray, bending shots. Once you do, you'll start hitting the ball more consistently, add distance and achieve better control. Before long, the game will be more enjoyable.

The following is a list of quick fixes to help you hit straighter, more consistent shots:

1. Think "Topspin" & "Thumbs Up"

Watching tennis can help your golf game. All skilled tennis players apply topspin to their shots by releasing or turning over their racket when they hit the ball. In golf, the move is similar, only it's made with a club in your hand. Allowing for the release of the hands is critical to maximizing your potential and reducing slices. The next time you're practicing, take a club and swing. As you pass the impact position, think of the right hand reaching out in front on the follow through with  your thumps pointing upward. This shows that the wrists rolled properly and the club was released.

2. Strengthen Your Grip

Chronic slicers have trouble getting their hands rotated through impact. Start by gripping the club in the fingers rather than the palm of your hand. At address, make sure you are able to see two or three knuckles of the left hand. This "strengthening" of the grip allows the hands to work actively.

3. Pull the Rope

Most slicers cut across the ball on the downswing. They take the club back to the outside on the backswing and cross their plane (imaginary line) to the inside on the downswing. This produces a slice. To understand the correct swing path or downswing motion, picture a rope attached to a tree above you. Now imagine yourself pulling that rope straight down. Take that thought with you to the driving range and try to pull your club straight down when starting the downswing. This also  forces the right elbow to stay close to your side - a key to not crossing the line. Practicing this gives you the correct inside path and a better ability to swing out toward the target.

4. Start Back to the Inside

Imagine the line of your swing on the ground as it goes back and through toward the target. Place a range basket, or other object you don't want to break, on the ground a couple of feet behind the ball and slightly inside the intended target line. Practicing this drill forces you to swing from the inside out toward the target - the proper way!

5. Shoulders Right to Hit Left

Most players aim farther and farther to the left to accommodate their slice. This only makes matters worse by opening the shoulders. Your swing plane tends to follow your shoulders. If they are open, your odds of cutting across the ball increase. Try doing just the opposite. Aim the shoulders as far to the right as possible at address. This forces the swing to stay on the proper path.

6. Swing around Your Spine

The best way to eliminate the typical slice, one that is caused by a reverse pivot or sway motion, is to swing your spine and finish around and to the left. Use "x-ray vision" - picture your spine remaining in a near-perpendicular angle to the ground at all times during the swing. Now, just swing around the center of it!

These tips work best if they're combined with each other. For instance, achieving the proper swing path won't prevent you from hitting to the right if you don't use your hands properly.

Practice each strategy separately in the beginning and then combine them. You'll soon be saying goodbye to your slice - forever!

Lesson 18: Playing From Various Bunker Lies

When attempting a bunker shot, most amateurs know to twist their feet into the sand. This is a good idea, but how you should do this varies depending on the lie. Ignoring different types of lies and ball positions in the sand sets you up for poor balance, slipping and an inability to control ball flight - not to mention higher scores!

Consistently practice the following footwork basics and watch your sand play become more predictable:

Ball below Feet: Use Less Lower Body

This is perhaps the toughest position because there is a tendency to fall forward during the swing and change your spine angle. Dig your heels into the slope and try to feel as though the weight is on the balls of your feet. You'll need a little more knee flex to keep you from topping the ball. Try to maintain the same amount of flex throughout the swing. Remember less is better when it comes to using leg and lower-body action - especially on this difficult shot!

Downhill Lies: Set Your Weight

Gravity forces most of your weight on the downhill or lower leg. Make sure to set your weight on the inside of the forward foot for more stability. I also recommend that you turn out your toe slightly to help absorb the extra weight transfer caused by gravity. Normally, you would open your stance considerably in the sand. However, on these shots, you have to be careful. If you open the stance, your right leg will be in the way of your swing. To avoid this, pull your back foot away a few inches.

Uphill Lies: Brace Yourself

With gravity working to keep your weight on the downhill leg, it's important to brace it firmly into the sand. Angle your leg into the slope so that the weight is on the inside of the downhill leg. When you swing, the weight will be easier to shift forward.

Ball above Feet: Adjust Your Aim

The first adjustment to make is to dig your toes in deeper than your heels. This helps keep you level and makes it easier to remain balanced. Keep the legs flexed. Aiming a bit to the right and using a slightly open stance is also recommended, as uphill lies tend to promote a hook or pulled shot.

Buried Lie: Use the Right Twist

The deeper you submerge your feet into the sand, the deeper the club enters the sand. Therefore, if the ball is only slightly buried, you don't need to twist in too deep. For a severely buried lie, twisting in to the approximate depth of the buried   lie helps you get under the ball. For this type of shot, you   need to pick up the club steeply and hit down and through   on a sharp U-like swing plane.

Obviously, the best advice is to stay out of these tough lies in the first place. But we all know that's easier said than done. Besides, this game wouldn't be any fun if it weren't challenging!

Lesson 19: Learning to Properly Release the Club

Many players have shared common problems - the inability to generate power and slicing the ball. In most instances, both of these problems stem from having a poor or improper release. This lesson lists ways to help you release or turn over the club.

Whether you want to gain a few extra yards or are just beginning and want to ingrain proper habits, put the following tips to work for better all-around ball striking:

Try a Split Grip

Perhaps the best drill to emphasize proper hand release is to grip the club so that you have a few inches of space between your hands. Next, make a few swings with the club going only half way back and through. Practicing this drill helps exaggerate the feeling of the right hand crossing over the left. When you do this properly, you'll see the toe of the club facing upward, both at hip height on the backswing and at hip height on the follow-through.

Don't Hold On

"Holding on" means that instead of being relaxed through impact, there is a tendency to grip too tightly and hold on - not releasing the full potential of the swing. When you anticipate the hit rather than swinging through the ball, there is inevitably a tendency to tighten and hold on too much. The most fluid way to swing is as though you aren't hitting the ball at all, but rather swinging through it.

Improve Your Posture

Ben Hogan once remarked, "Ninety percent of a golf shot - good or bad - occurs before the swing." Start by standing very erect with your back flat. Flex the knees and push your behind out so that your knees are roughly above the balls of the feet. Try to maintain this position as you bend over from the waist. Think of the arms and hands being low and relaxed as though gravity is pulling them straight down. Now stand at address with a club. Make sure that an angle is  established with the wrists. This angle is important because you are lessening the moving parts of your swing by setting the wrist cock in advance. This allows for a hinging action of the wrists and makes it much easier to release the club on the follow-through. Quite often, beginner golfers reach too much for the ball. This causes the wrists to roll in the swing, rather than hinge and unhinge.

Relax Your Grip Pressure

Start by determining your grip pressure. How tight are you gripping the club on a scale of 1-10, with 10 being as tight as you can squeeze and 1 being not holding on at all? Generally, the best players grip about a 6 on this scale. Any tighter and tension gets in the way, going all the way up the arms and into the upper body. Too much grip tension inhibits the lag (delayed hit) and release motions that are critical to extension and a full release of the hands and arms. After you have set a light but firm pressure, monitor the consistency throughout the swing. Is it the same throughout, or does it tighten or loosen somewhere during the swing? Keeping a light pressure consistently allows you the freedom to make the correct move. Remember, the tighter you grip the club, the less your hands work in unison, and the more they inhibit your release.

Develop a Pre-Shot Routine

Being tight in the body and with the grip aren't the only things that affect your game and release. Your mind must also remain clear and focused. Start by using a consistent pre-shot routine. This routine should allow you to relax and visualize positive results. Developing a pre-shot routine can clear the mind so you're free to go ahead and give the ball your best shot.

Drop the Right Foot Back

Dropping the right foot back as you take some swings helps you to swing along a path that allows for a full hand release. Drop the right foot back about one foot at address, and try to swing across your body with easy swings. After you get the feeling of your hands being able to release, trick yourself - retain the motion while slowly moving the foot back into the normal position.

Use the Big Muscles

To generate your full power potential, you must use your trunk and midsection. Any athlete, from boxer to baseball pitcher, will agree that their power starts from the legs, trunk and midsection. This is where the big muscles are located and where you must rely for a smoother motion. Practice feeling that the belly button is facing the target at the end of the swing and that you finish the swing balanced on the right toe. To fully release the hips, weight must get off the left foot and up onto the toe. If you make a good body release combined with the hand release, you'll wonder where all that power was stored!

One of the biggest breakthroughs you will feel in golf is when your **body and hands release their energy at the same time.** When this is happening, the right elbow stays close to the right side - almost touching the hip - as both it and the hips move or release through that poor golf ball. This is called efficient use of energy and it comes only through practice.

Lesson 20: Learn To Transfer Your Weight

It seems like it should be easy: Start the swing with the weight evenly distributed on both feet and finish with it on the left foot and right toe. After all, we do this every time we take a step and in almost any sport. Proper weight transfer is necessary to powerfully propel an object. Yet, many golfers often try to help the ball get up in the air by hitting up or at it.

The following lesson will help you understand some of the ways to hit through the ball with a correct weight shift:

Understand Weight Shift

Students often find it hard to understand and feel their weight shift. A good way to begin is to close your eyes and take a few practice swings. Afterwards, give each foot a percentage weighting for the beginning at address, middle and end of the swing. If you're swinging properly, the beginning or address position should feel like your weight is evenly distributed between your left and right feet on a flat lie. At the top of the backswing, if you've made a good turn without swaying, it should feel like 80% of your weight is on the inside of your right foot and 20% is on the inside of your left foot. The follow-through should feel exactly the opposite. If these closed-eye swings aren't close to these numbers, try the following drills:

Walk Through the Shot

Take your normal address position and swing a club to the top of the **backswing.** As you come down and through the ball, make an effort to step forward after you've made contact, as if you are walking. Gary Player made this move famous and still does it on many shots. This drill and position emphasizes that you've made a good weight shift.

You "Can" Do It

Place an object such as a soda can about a foot behind your ball. Using a short-iron, try to hit your ball without hitting the can. You'll notice that you're forced to come down at a steeper angle. By swinging with this steeper angle, you're also forced to shift properly off the right foot and take a divot in front of the ball. When you don't, you'll find yourself hitting behind the ball or topping it. This is often the result of hanging back on the right foot. After a few swings, try placing that same object in front of the ball about 2 feet. The goal is to swing out over the can as low as possible on the follow-through without actually hitting it. This extension drill promotes a strong weight shift to the left leg and gets you to hit through, rather than at, your ball. This is great if you often top the ball.

Swing On a Slope

To feel weight shift happening naturally, try swinging while standing on a downhill or uphill slope. On a downhill slope, gravity pushes your weight toward the front foot, making it easier to finish the swing with the weight fully transferred. When doing this, keep your shoulder line fairly parallel with the slope of the ground to avoid hitting behind the ball.

Keep Your Weight Inside

Keeping your weight on the inside of the right foot during the backswing is critical to shifting properly. Allowing the weight to get to the outside of the foot doesn't give you a strong base to push off from when "springing" over to the left side. This can also lead to the dreaded sway. This results in a lot of wasted movement and is detrimental to good swing mechanics. To find a proper position, keep the right knee over the inside of the foot at address and throughout the

backswing. Obviously, it's not helpful to think about this during the swing. However, stop at the top of the swing occasionally and check your position. In time, this will pay off in added power and more solid hits.

There are many more ways to drill the concept of weight shifting inside. However, you must first learn how it feels and start noticing what's going on throughout your swing. After you can do that, you will see the correlation between solid shots and good shifting. This is how the pros make it look so easy, yet hit it so far. Also try getting that right toe of your golf shoe dirty. This is a good sign of fully shifting and turning.

As always, don't forget to have fun!

Lesson 21: Learn to Check Your Alignment

When it comes to fundamentals, you'll often hear about grip, posture and ball position. Although all of these are important to building a consistent swing, alignment is the most critical. You can have the best swing in the world. However, if you're not properly aligned with the target, you'll hit the ball anywhere.

Imagine trying to sink a pool ball in the pocket without aiming. You'd really have to manipulate that pool cue on the forward stroke in order to get the ball on line wouldn't you? The same is true in golf, so why make a difficult game more complex?

The majority of amateurs align too far to the right, setting themselves up for the familiar "over-the-top" swing in an effort to get the ball on line. The result is usually a pull, a slice, or glancing contact with the ball.

The main alignment check points are the feet, knees, hips and shoulders. Unless you're making a conscious effort to draw or fade the ball, these points should all be consistent and parallel to the target line.

Start Behind the Ball

The first step in your pre-shot routine is to get directly behind the ball and draw an imaginary line from your ball to your target. Although you'll see most pros do this on TV, you will seldom see amateurs taking this approach. This allows you to get a good sense of target and to visualize a positive ball flight.

Square the Clubface to the Target

Pick a spot such as a leaf or divot in front of the ball that's on the same imaginary target line you saw when you stood behind the ball. As you set up, align the clubface perpendicular to that spot. Another way is to line up the label on the ball toward the target and then the clubface. Check yourself often, as this is an area that requires a great deal of precision.

Place Clubs on the Ground

One of the most effective ways to train proper alignment is to place 2 clubs in a parallel position on the ground. Start by aiming the first club directly at the flag and another parallel to it, approximately where your feet would be. Laying clubs on the ground is also a great way to spot-check how you're doing. If you set up in what you think is the correct position and lay down the clubs once in a while, it will allow you to catch poor habits early. Remember, if the feet are to the right of the target, you'll have a harder time clearing the left hip and using the legs properly. This drill ensures perfect aim.

Check Your Shoulder Position

As you look back and forth toward the flag - verifying your aim - there's a tendency to leave the shoulders open. This will prove counterproductive to an otherwise good position. To check this last area, try placing a club on the line of the shoulders with the grip end facing the flag. If you extend the line of where the grip is pointing, you'll get a good indication of direction. By doing this, you can also ensure the shoulder line is pointing in the same direction as the line on which your feet are aimed.

As you can see, alignment is imperative. Without it, you could swing and hit the ball like Tiger Woods, but never make a birdie or hit a green.

Lesson 22: Adopting Proper Putting Fundamentals

After seeing numerous putting styles, we have come to the conclusion that the majority of great golfers use the same putting fundamentals. Some of these are physical and some are mental. Very little of the so-called "magic" actually comes from a **putter,** but rather from the confidence within the player.

Think Positive

Positive thinking can represent the doorway to good putting. Remember a time when you were putting well. It probably felt as though you couldn't miss, and you had a greater belief that the ball would go in. Positive feelings and visualization are the key. This belief comes from prior success and success comes from solid fundamentals and practice.

Grip for Success

Hold the hands close enough together so that they work as a unit, rather than independently. When they're separate, there's a better chance of the wrists breaking down, which leads to inconsistency. A popular grip used by many tour players is a reverse overlap that takes the forefinger of the left hand off the putter and rests it on the little finger of the right hand. A cross-handed grip is also worth trying if you break the wrists during the stroke. Equally important is grip pressure. Aim for light pressure rather than tight pressure because tightness diminishes feel.

Consider Ball Position

The left eye should be directly over the ball at address. This means that the ball is placed forward in the stance, off the inside of the left foot. This also gives you a much better perspective of your putt's intended line of travel.

Keep the Putter Moving

Accelerate the putter toward the hole. Practice some short putts about one foot from the hole and try rolling the ball and putter right over the hole. Remember, the follow-through should exceed the backstroke. You can ensure this by placing another ball behind the ball you're hitting on the practice green. As you make the backstroke, stop when you hit the second ball.

Have the Right Distance

Standing too far from the ball causes an improper stroke path - one that makes too much of an arc from the inside so that it's difficult for the face to be square to the target. Conversely, if you stand too close, you tend to force the backstroke outside of the target line. When making these mistakes, it forces you to manipulate the putter to square it at impact.

Locate he Hands Ahead

Locating your hands forward is another fundamental common to good putting techniques. If your hands are behind the ball, there's a tendency to add loft to the putt and break your wrists. By keeping your hands up front and even with the ball or slightly ahead, you'll ensure a better roll.

Lock the Body

Keep body movement minimal. Good players putt while keeping their bodies locked in position for the entire stroke. Doing this allows the shoulders, rather than the hips, to dominate the movement. A great way to check how solid you are is to use the sun's shadow. Putt with the shadow facing in front of you so you can detect any lateral movement. Place a ball or club on the green at the outer edges of the shadow of your hips. As you take some practice strokes, pay attention and see if you can detect any movement. You can also practice this shadow trick to ensure your head and shoulders stay in place and don't sway.

If you can blend these key fundamental with your own style, you'll find that your putts will start to fall more frequently.

Lesson 23: Getting Your Total Game in Shape

Playing good golf involves a lot more than just beating around countless balls on the driving range. If you really want to get the most from the sport, you must **concentrate your efforts on several key areas** that help make your game complete and keep you on track.

Let's explore the following areas that have the biggest impact on your game:

Practice Makes Perfect

There is no point investing in swing instruction if you can't learn to repeat what you learned. Remember, a golf teacher is only responsible for part of the picture. Repetition breeds confidence and confidence breeds success. There is no substitute for practice. Practice must be performed with purpose and then complemented with play.

Get Professional Instruction

Receiving professional instruction on a regular basis is vital to keeping your game on track. So often, we think we can solve our game problems without help. This can sometimes result in making a simple problem worse. A check up by a golf instructor can make a huge difference. Remember, a well-trained professional eye can see things that you can't.

Get Out There & Do It

Playing the game of golf is what it's all about. It's hard to perfect your technique and implement all the advice you read, unless you get on the course often. Practice and play with purpose and measure the results.

Think Positive

This is often an overlooked part of the game even though it accounts for so much. Listen to the **self-talk in your head**. Are you hard on yourself? Do you adopt a "poor me" attitude? When you really listen to your inner self, you'll be amazed at what you hear. Try to maintain a positive outlook while on the course. The more confident your thoughts are, the more confident your play. Before long, your scores will drop. Golf may be one of the greatest games ever devised - it combines all the elements of balance and strength with both body and mind.

The Right Stuff

Who needs custom clubs? An easy response would be "everyone." However, certain players tend to reap greater rewards than others by using custom clubs. These players commonly have unique body features. For example, they might have short or long fingers, a tall body with relatively short arms, or a short body with relatively long arms. Everyone is unique. Remember, don't adjust your game to a set of clubs - adjust your clubs to your game.

Fit Your Game

Compose the set of the clubs you are most efficient using. There's no point carrying a 2-iron if you can't get it up in the air and don't feel confident using it. Instead, opt for a **5 or 7-wood.** Many Senior Tour and women professionals do this. Even players such as Nick Faldo have been seen carrying high-lofted fairway woods in their bag. Because the rules allow for 14 clubs only, fill your bag with ones you use most often and most efficiently.

If taking your game up a notch is important to you, review this short list and make sure you give each area appropriate attention. The results could take you up to the next level!

Lesson 24: Getting Out Of Trouble Spots

During the course of a round, you'll often find yourself in situations that require specialty shots to get out of trouble. Most of the time, a hook or slice can be the worst thing in the world. However, there may be times when you need to deliberately hit such a shot. In fact, the ability to choose your type of shot depending on the situation is what transforms average golfers into great golfers.

This lesson describes different types of shots and the easiest ways to hit them:

Hook

For right-handed golfers, a hook curves from right to left. This shot tends to roll farther than a sliced shot. To hit a hook, the clubface must be closed in

relation to the target line at impact. The simplest way to hit this shot is to start with a normal stance and grip, and direct the clubface toward the target. Then pull back the right or back foot a few inches, so that the line of your feet is aiming to the right of the target 10-15 yards. Aligning your feet this way forces you to swing on an inside-to-outside plane. At impact, this swing path puts a counterclockwise spin on the ball and makes it hook. This technique coupled with a closed clubface produces an even bigger hook. If you're having trouble, ensure there's a feeling of the hands rolling over through impact. For a more pronounced hook, manipulate your grip. Rotate your hands more to the right at address.

Slice

You can hit a slicing shot many ways. The simplest way to slice on purpose is to reverse the procedure you followed for the hook. Pull the left foot back so your stance points to the left. Leave the clubface pointed toward the target and swing across on the new feet line. You can add more slice by "weakening" the grip. Rotate the hands and grip position to the left. When you hit a slice, there's less hand action and rotation through the ball.

Fade & Draw

A fade is a mild version of a slice and a draw is a mild version of a hook. Because hitting the ball dead straight every time is so difficult, good players incorporate slight nuances of the hook or slice; they attempt to make one of these ball flights their "bread & butter" shot. This way, they know the direction the ball is curving, allowing for greater control and course management. Jack Nicklaus has always said the best way to hit a fade  is to slightly open your clubface at address and take a normal swing. To hit a draw, slightly close the clubface at address and take your usual swing.

High Shot

Hitting high shots can be valuable in situations where the greens are very firm or you need to get the ball over a high object such as a tree. This type of shot lands softer, allowing golfers to carry over bunkers and still keep the ball close to the flag. Start by placing the ball slightly more forward in the stance than normal. Then visualize your spine angle being vertical to the ground at address. When you approach impact on the swing, your spine angle can be at a slightly upward or "launch" angle. You achieve this best by ensuring your head stays back through the shot. It's OK to shift the weight of your lower body, but force your upper body to stay back. A more upright swing plane promotes a higher ball flight.

Low Shot

Low shots are fun to hit, especially into wind or under trees. Place the ball farther back in the stance compared to your normal ball position. As you come through impact, there are two positions to feel. First, make sure that the hands have stayed in front of the ball, keeping the loft of the club low. Second, ensure the spine angle is still vertical rather than a typical launch angle. A shorter backswing often helps here as well. This position gives you a nice controlled low shot. The shot tends to roll more, so plan accordingly.

These are just a few of the many creative shots you can learn to produce in an imaginative round of golf.

Lesson 25: The Art of the Bump & Run

As the old saying goes, there are many ways to get the ball in the hole. While this is certainly true, the majority of good players realize that specific types of shots are more effective and consistent than others. Conventional wisdom indicates that it's best not to loft the ball any more than necessary. Nonetheless, many players insist on hitting lofted or lob shots when they aren't necessary. These lofted shots are much more difficult to control than the good old "bump and run."

If you have ever watched the British Open, you have certainly seen a bump and run. A bump and run is a shot that lands over the fringe less than a third of the way to the hole and then rolls or "runs" the rest of the way. This shot is ideal in windy, firm conditions or when no bunkers are guarding the front of the green. On shorter distances, it's almost as though you are "bumping" the ball gently onto the putting surface and letting it run the rest of the way. Both club selection and technique are important in pulling off this shot.

Practice This Drill

One of the biggest destroyers of consistency around the green is overuse of the wrists. When they break down through impact, it opens the door to a chipping nightmare. For the bump and run (and nearly all shots around the green), position the hands slightly in front of the ball at address. The hands should also reach impact in this position and through to the finish. To aid in this, play the ball slightly back of the middle of your stance.

A good way to ensure the correct hand position is to have a friend place the grip end of a club slightly in front of the ball as you begin your downswing. As you swing, let your club hit the grip end of the club on the ground, stopping your forward progress. This forces your hands to stay ahead of the ball.

Position the Shaft on Your Wrist

Grip your club all the way down - below the grip and on the shaft - so there's enough of the grip above your hands to rest it on your left forearm as you simulate the address position. In this position, your club will be well above the ground, so you can't hit the ball. Now, take some practice strokes. If the club's grip stays connected to the left forearm on the follow-through of your pretend chip shot, it's good. If it slips off your forearm, it's an indication

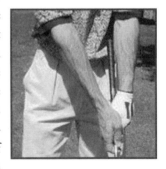

there's too much wrist use. Do this until you can keep the grip from disconnecting.

Pick the Right Stick

Many players use the same club for all low-trajectory shots. This isn't the most effective method. For more predictability, you should change clubs depending on the lie, the slope, green speed and various other factors. That way, you can use the same stroke every time - only changing the loft of the club, rather than having to change the technique for each shot. Good club selection also requires imagination; you should make it a priority to visualize each shot before you attempt it. Picture where you want the ball to land (always in the first third of the green with two thirds being in roll), and then choose the club that will give the desired loft.

Practice the low-trajectory shot on a flat area. Use the same stroke on every shot while alternating clubs - 6-iron all the way down to a pitching wedge. Pay close attention to how high the ball goes and how much roll each club produces.

Point Your Watch toward the Target

This is an old drill that really works. Simply imagine the back of the left wrist or your watch facing the target. As you follow through, keep the face of your watch directed at the target. It will be natural for it to turn over to the left or face upward as you go through the ball. However, resist and keep pointing that wrist toward the target - and toward better chipping.

BAD SHOTS IN GOLF

For a high-handicap golfer, hitting bad shots is quite common. This is understandable since inexperienced golfers don't have a sound swing. With practice, the bad shots will eventually disappear. Some players will eradicate these bad shots very quickly, whereas others may take longer. Identifying bad shots and what causes them can hasten your quest to eliminate them.

A bad shot is a shot whose behavior is not what you wanted. The main cause of hitting a bad shot is incorrect contact of the clubface with your ball.

Here are some common bad shots:

Fat Shot

A fat shot occurs when your clubhead hits the ground before hitting the ball. The ground slows down your swing speed considerably. Your ball flies into the air for a short while and then drops quickly to the ground.

Try to change the position of your ball in your stance. Usually you can gauge the position with some practice swings made near the ball. Stand in a position that will allow you to hit the ball first instead of the ground.

Shank Shot

This is a really bad shot. A shank is where the side of your club hits the ball instead of the clubface. This happens when you sent your clubhead too far away from your body. The shank is a dangerous shot because the ball takes off at a right angle towards you. You can get hit by your own ball!

To cure the shank shot, try standing further from the ball. A slower and more relaxed swing will also help.

Slice Shot

The slice is a very common bad shot for beginners. Your ball travels from left to right, traveling farther and farther away from your target. A slice is caused by an open clubface resulting from an out-to-in swing.

An immediate cure is to close your clubface slightly at address. This will compensate the out-to-in swing. A better way is to correct your out-to-in swing by keeping your right arm closer to your body during the downswing.

Hook Shot

The hook is the opposite of the slice. Your ball travels from right to left, moving farther and farther left of the target. The cause is the opposite of the slice; your swing travels in an in-to-out direction resulting in a closed clubface upon contact with the ball. A hook shot rolls more than a slice shot. If you consistently hit a hook shot, try hitting a slice. This may compensate for your hook.

Fade Shot

A mild form of the slice is the fade. A fade isn't actually a bad shot because it's controllable. Many golfers, including pros, often play this shot intentionally.

Push Shot

A push shot is a straight shot that travels to the right of the target instead of toward it. The direction of your swing causes this shot. You contact the ball squarely, but your swing isn't along the target line. Make sure your clubface travels along the target line to eliminate the push shot.

Pull Shot

The opposite of the push shot is the pull shot. Your ball flies straight to the left of the target. Again, the cause is the direction of your swing. The cure is to swing along the target line.

Top Shot

A top shot is when the ball hardly leaves the ground. This happens when your clubface contacts the top of the ball. To cure a top shot, concentrate on hitting the back of the ball. Shifting your weight to the front will also help.

Sometimes, when a ball is hit near the top, it may fly at a few feet above the ground for a considerable distance and then continue to roll.

This shot is called a "worm burner".

Chili-Dip

A fat shot hit near the green is called a chili-dip. As always, keep your eyes focused on the ball when you are near the green.

MORE SHORT GAME TIPS

The short game makes up more than 70% of golf, hence we spend a bit more time on it. Driving the ball is fun, but the real talent shows when you are less than 100 yards from the pin. Below are the components of the short game:

Pitching

A pitch shot is used to send the ball on the green at a distance from 40- 90 yards.

Here are the steps:

1. Stand with a slightly open stance with the ball towards your right foot.

2. Keep your left arm straight and in front of the ball.

3. Your weight should be on your left side all the time.

4. Make a smooth, full swing initiated by your arms, not your lower body.

5. Keep your shoulders square and your left arm straight.

6. Flex your right knee towards the target.

7. Maintain the back of your left hand facing the target for a longer period.

8. Your follow-through should be a mirror-image of your backswing.

The aim of a pitch shot is to land on the green with as little roll as possible.

Chipping

When your ball is less than 40 yards, a chip shot is used. Basically, there are two ways of chipping your ball onto the green:

Bump & Run – a ball that flies low, bumps on the green and runs a long way.

You can use nearly the entire range of irons, depending on the flag location.

- Use an open stance

- Play the ball way back

- Hood the clubface to slightly reduce its loft

- Use a putting arm and shoulder movement

- Strike downward, hitting the ball and ground at the same time

- Sweep through the ball along the target line

- Follow through and keep your eyes on the ball

Flop Shot – a ball that flies high and lands with little roll. When there is water or a bunker in front of the green, a flop shot is used. Use a sand wedge or lob wedge (60%) for this shot.

- Start with an open stance

- Ball position should be at the middle or slightly ahead of middle of stance

- Open up your clubface and aim at the target

- Swing your arms lazily along your body line

- Slide the clubface under the ball keeping the clubface facing the sky

- Keep your arms moving through the shot

The key to a successful flop is a slow and easy tempo. Trying the flop on a hardpan is risky.

Sand Play

Sooner or later, you will find yourself in the sand bunker. Actually, bunkers shots are easier than you think. This is one time you don't even have to hit the ball. You are hitting the sand behind the ball which gives you a bigger margin of error!

Here is how you do it:

- Choose the sand wedge for a greenside bunker.

- Gauge your distance from the target.

- Plant your feet firmly. Wriggling your feet into the sand will give you an idea of its firmness.

- Use an open stance. Taking the target line as 12 o'clock, your feet should line up at 11 o'clock.

- Offset your clubface to 1 o'clock to counter your open stance.

- Open your clubface to face the sky as in the flop shot. For wet or hard sand, square your stance and close your clubface.

- Swing along your body line keeping your body still.

- Your club must strike the sand 2-3 inches behind the ball. The less sand you take, the more spin you put on the ball. Less sand also means greater risk.

- Keep your wrists firm throughout and well after impact.

- A steep downswing angle will yield a shorter distance, while a shallow angle will hit the ball longer.

The above instructions are for a normal sand shot. However, your ball may end up in some tricky situations. Such conditions may call for a slight variation.

Below are some possible scenarios:

- **In A Footprint** – You find your ball inside a footprint left by someone else. The solution is to play the ball as a **lob shot**. You may need to switch to a pitching wedge or a 9-iron.

- **In A Downhill Lie** – Your ball is lying at the back of the bunker in a downhill position. You need to take more sand at the back of the ball. Close the clubface more to suit the contour. Play the ball off your right heel to promote a steeper entry angle.

- **In An Uphill Lie** – Your ball is in front of the bunker in an uphill lie. Since the terrain is uphill, your club will dig deeper into the sand. In this situation, hit closer to the ball with a stronger follow-through. Play an out-to-in cut shot. Your clubface should remain open and square to the line of flight.

- **On Top Of Firm Level Sand With No Overhanging Lip** – This is a rare situation. Use your putter and a flat-arm motion to keep your clubhead parallel to the sand. Keep your body weight on your left foot.

Buried Bunker Lie – If the sand is soft, the ball may become embedded.

If you are thinking of a bigger swing with a bigger follow-through, you'll be in big trouble. The laws of the usual bunker shot don't apply to this situation.

Here is what you should do:

- Your stance should be a bit squarer than the usual bunker stance.

- The clubface should also be squarer.

- Have a steep backswing.

- Strike the leading edge of the clubface into the sand 1-3 inches behind the ball. You can swing hard.

- Do NOT follow through.

The ball will pop out of the sand with little or no spin.

"Knowing the basics of sand play takes away your fear; knowing the subtleties will actually lead you to enjoy playing from bunkers."

- Greg Norman

More about Ball Positions

So far, you have been taught to play the ball from off the heel of your left foot. You can hit the ball at the bottom of your swing all the time. You are consistently getting a clean square hit.

Now try this scenario. You find yourself about 130 yards from the green. Your 7-iron is too strong and your 8-iron is not strong enough. You don't want to choke down on the 7-iron.

What do you do?

Use your 8-iron.

This is where you change your ball position. In your normal ball position (A), your 8-iron's loft will send your ball too high where it can't reach the green. However, if you move your left leg a little in front, you will no longer be hitting the ball at the bottom of your swing. Your clubface will come into contact with the ball at a descending angle. The loft in this position (B) is less than the club's loft at A, thus sending the ball lower and further.

The opposite happens when you move the ball forward or move your left foot backwards. Your clubhead is at its lowest point and on its way up. You are catching the ball on an upswing of the club. This increases the loft angle (C) and sends the ball higher into the air.

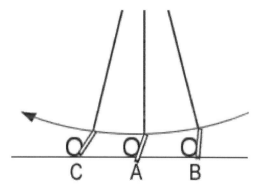

The balls in this diagram are far apart to show you the loft angles of each club.

In real life, you don't have to move that far forward or backwards. You don't have to alter your swing. Just a minor change in ball position will give your ball a new flight height and distance. This will open up a whole new game!

Putting

Hole	1	2	3	4	5	6	7	8	9	Total
Par	4	5	4	4	3	5	3	4	4	36
Driver	1	1	0	1	0	1	0	1	1	6
Long Irons	1	1	1	0	1	1	1	0	1	7
Mid Irons	0	1	1	1	0	1	0	1	1	6
Short Irons	1	1	0	1	1	2	1	1	0	8
Putter	2	2	2	2	2	1	2	2	2	17

The table above indicates how many times a typical bogey player used his clubs during the first 9 holes of his round. A glance at his putter usage reveals him to be a skilled putter. He never one three-putted which is a feat even the pros would admire.

In the round of 9 holes, this golfer used his putter 17 times. This is more than twice the number of times he used any other equipment! This shows how important putting is to the game of golf. Therefore, it makes sense to invest time in this aspect of the game. Many golfers spend time at the range practicing their driving and irons, but they don't spend serious time on the practice green.

Putting is called a game within a game because the skills involved are different from the rest of the game. Putting really lives up to the adage "Drive for show; Putt for dough". You can have the most spectacular drive in the round.

However, that's not going to show in the scorecard.

If your putting is no good, you will probably end up buying the beers!

Here are five simple steps to help you become a better putter:

1. Position – Stand in a position so that your eyes are over the line of putt. Your left eye should be directly over the ball. To test if this is done correctly, hold the putter loosely and directly under your eyes and let it hang straight down. As you look down, does the putter cover the ball? If not, move forward or backward.

Now that your ball is directly under your left eye, your hands should remain a little forward of the ball. The putter shaft should be aligned with your left forearm. This gives a good roll to the ball.

2. Grip – The putting stroke is done with no wrist movement. Your hands, arms and shoulder should work together as a unit. Let your shoulder direct the movement of the club. Grip the club lightly to promote a better feel.

3. Aim – Find a target to aim your ball. If the hole is close enough and the ground is level, make it your target. If the hole is on a slope, the target should be the point where your ball will make its turn. This is called the apex. Imagine a straight line from there to the middle of your putter.

Unlike the full swing, your leg alignment is not as important in putting. What is important is your putter face remaining square to the target line. This is the line your putter should follow.

4. Stroke – You putting stroke involves only your shoulders and arms. Forget about the rest of the body. Keep them as still as possible, especially your head. Focus on contacting the ball when your swing is ascending to encourage a more forward roll. A forward rolling ball stays on line longer.

5. Acceleration – The purest stroke in putting is the pendulum stroke. The backswing and follow-through are of equal length. Deceleration is the worst enemy of putting. Stroke through the ball, not at it.

Nerves are the next biggest enemy. When the entire match depends on that final three-foot putt, you will discover just what we mean. Even the pros can succumb to a bout of nerves.

Next time you visit the practice green, try sinking in three-foot putts with your eyes closed. Closing your eyes makes you feel the putting stroke. Since you aren't looking at anything, you won't feel as nervous.

Reading the Green

In order to be a good putter, you must be able to read the putting green.

Reading the green is a combination of proper putting techniques including a good putting swing and knowing where to aim and target your ball. Before you take out your putter and swing, you need to read the green. In this section, we'll provide some guidelines on reading the green:

- **Slope Of The Green** – The slope of the green will affect both the speed and direction. There are only two angles to read. The first is the up-down angle. You see this angle from the side or from an angle perpendicular to the line of putt. You want to determine whether your ball is lying below or above the hole. If the ball is below, you need to hit harder and vice versa.

  The next angle is the left-right angle. You see this angle along the line of putt or behind the ball. Some golfers hold their putter at eye level for a better view.

  Angles become more complicated when more than one slope is involved.

- **Grass Length** – The simple formula is common sense. Grass causes resistance. Therefore, the longer the grass, the more resistance. This means the ball will roll slower.

- **Firmness** – Treat firmness as hardness. A hard surface has less resistance than a soft surface. Therefore, the firmer the green, the faster the roll. Warning: You aren't allowed to press your putter on the ground to test for firmness.

- **Moisture** – Moisture also causes resistance. More moisture means more resistance. Wet grass can really slow a ball down.

- **Direction Of Grass** – See which way the grass is pointing or the grain. Your ball will roll slower against the grain than along the grain.

- **Type Of Grass** – Your ball will travel faster on Bent grass than on Bermuda. You don't have to worry about grains with Bent grass.

- **Wind** – Just like in the air, wind also affects your ball on the ground. Your ball will roll faster with the wind and slower against the wind.

Observing the behavior of another golfer's ball will provide some idea of the green's characteristics. This is even more apparent if the golfer's line of putt is close to yours. However, it's not considered proper etiquette to stand in front or behind a golfer when he is putting.

Bear in mind that this reading only applies if your ball is more than 4 feet from the hole. If your ball is within 4 feet of the hole, you should forget about wind, grain or firmness. Unless the slope is really severe, you should even forget about the slope. Just aim for the back of the cup and firmly stroke the ball. At this distance, the momentum will send the ball into the cup before any of the above factors come into play.

TROUBLESHOOTING

Diagnosing the Push Shot

Characteristics

Your ball starts to the right for a right-handed golfer and continues to fly straight along that line of flight. You will find your ball right of the target. If you look at the divot you make, it will also point to the right.

Below is a checklist of possible causes of the push shot. See which one correctly describes your fault and make the necessary adjustments:

Checklist:

Grip: Not a factor here.

Ball position: Your ball is placed too far back in your stance. You hit the ball before your clubhead reaches the bottom of the swing.

Stance: Your stance is too wide.

Body alignment : Your feet, hips and shoulders are pointing too far to the right.

Posture: Your body weight is back on your heels instead of forward on the balls of your feet.

Swing:

- On your backswing, you're taking the club back too far inside. This will pull your club away from the target line.

- On your downswing, your club is swinging toward the right and your head is following that direction.

- You drop your head before you start your downswing.

- Your hips are sliding towards the target instead of turning.

Shock Tactics for Practice: The next time you visit a driving range, choose the rightmost bay. Try hitting balls to the left side of the range.

Diagnosing the Pull Shot

Characteristics

Your ball starts out flying left of the target and continues to fly along that line.

Below is a checklist of possible causes of the pull shot. See which one correctly describes your fault and make the necessary adjustments:

Checklist:

Grip: Both your hands are twisted too far to your right making too strong a grip. This closes your clubface at impact.

Ball position: Your ball is too far forward in your stance.

Stance: Your stance is too narrow making the shoulders dominate the forward swing.

Body alignment : Your body alignment is pointing too far left.

Posture: Not enough knee flex.

Swing:

- You push your club towards the outside of the target line on your backswing.

- Your club is over your head at the top of your backswing when it should be over your shoulder.

- You are pushing your arms away from your body during the transition.

- You move your head toward the target during your downswing.

Shock Tactics for Practice: Open your clubface during backswing and close it after you hit the shot.

Diagnosing the Slice

Characteristics

Your ball starts to the left of the target and half way it starts to turn right until it finishes well right of the target.

Below is a checklist of possible causes of the slice. See which one correctly describes your fault and make the necessary adjustments:

Checklist:

Grip: Your left hand is turned too far to the left resulting in a weak grip. This causes your club to become open at impact.

Ball position: You position the ball to far forward.

Stance: Your stance is too narrow which causes instability.

Body alignment: Your body alignment is pointing too far left of the target. This will cause an "out-to-in" swing.

Posture: You are standing too far from the ball.

Swing:

- You are taking the clubhead too far to the outside on your backswing

- Your shoulder is going out instead of down, resulting in your arms being pushed away from you as you swing down. This causes an out-to-in swing

- Your wrist is blocking your club from turning over.

- You are relying too much on your arms instead of your hips.

Shock Tactics for Practice: Find a side hill lie and place balls above your feet. Practice hitting on this lie which will help you swing along the correct line.

Diagnosing the Unwanted Fade

The fade is a good technique to have and can prove useful when the situation warrants. However, some golfers tend to hit a fade all the time. This is a problem because a fade produces less distance.

If you consistently hit a fade, look at the following checklist to determine the cause:

Checklist:

Grip: Both your hands are twisted too far to your right making too strong a grip. This closes your clubface at impact.

Ball position: Your ball is too far forward in your stance.

Stance: Your stance is too narrow making the shoulders dominate the forward swing.

Body alignment : Your body alignment is pointing too far left.

Posture: Not enough knee flex.

Swing:

- You push your club towards the outside of the target line on your backswing.

- Your club is over your head at the top of your backswing when it should be over your shoulder.

- You are pushing your arms away from your body during the transition.

- You move your head toward the target during your downswing.

Shock Tactics for Practice: Open your clubface during backswing and close it after you hit the shot.

Diagnosing & Curing the Hook

Characteristics

Your ball starts to the right of the target, curves to the left and finishes to the left of the target. A hook devastates golfers more than any other shot.

Below is a checklist of possible causes. Find your fault and make the necessary adjustments:

Checklist:

Grip: Your left hand is turned too far to the right.

The "V" formed by your thumb and forefinger should point between your right shoulder and right ear, not outside your shoulder.

You shouldn't see more than 2 knuckles on your left hand.

Ball position: Your ball may be too far back in your stance.

Stance: Your stance may be too wide.

Body alignment: Your shoulders and feet are aligned too far right of the target.

Swing: It's not easy to hook a ball unless you're doing something drastic:

You are taking the club back too far inside during your backswing. Look at your club at the end of your backswing. Your shaft should be over your shoulder, not behind it.

- You begin your downswing by a counter-clockwise action, closing the clubface. This is the most probable cause for most golfers.

   On your backswing the turning of your shoulders should 'open' your clubface, not the twisting of your hands.

- During the downswing, your shoulder is lowering too much, accompanied with a sliding of your hips toward the target. You should start your downswing by shifting your weight to your left foot and turning your body.

- You are muscling the swing. Make sure your hands and arms are relaxed.

- You are directing the club too much to the right at impact. Try to keep the club moving at the target line.

Shock Tactics for Practice: Try to keep the clubface open all the way.

Topping the Ball

Topping the ball occurs when your clubhead contacts the ball above its equator.

What are the causes?

1. During set-up, your body is tilted. When you are about to hit the ball, your body rises. This causes the clubhead to rise up as well which results in topping.

2. During set-up, your arms are straight. When you are about to hit the ball, your arms are bent. This shortens the swing arc and contacts the ball higher up.

Is there a cure? Yes. A simple one.

First ask yourself the following question. What makes you raise your body or bend your arms? Most times it's because you want to crush the ball. You're trying to hit the ball too hard.

The cure is to relax. Don't swing so hard. Never swing at more than 80% of your full strength.

Casting

Have you ever wondered why that skinny lady can hit the ball farther than you? Her movements seem so smooth and effortless, yet her drive travels 10 yards farther than yours.

You don't have to be a hulk to hit a long ball. The trick is the wrist snap that gives the extra oomph to your swing. Timing is very important.

Many short hitters do not fully hinge their wrists. More short hitters snap their wrists too early on the downswing. This is called casting, and it's similar to a fisherman casting his rod. The result of casting is a loss of clubhead speed. You can make solid contact, but your ball will lack the extra kick to propel it farther.

For that extra kick, you must delay your wrist snap until the very last moment.

The answer is your right hand. Your right hand must hinge at, or just before, the top of your backswing. As you swing down, your hand must remain hinged until the last moment.

Before we proceed further, we need to distinguish between the two wrist

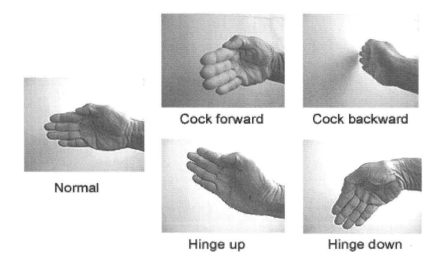

Cock forward   Cock backward

Normal

Hinge up   Hinge down

actions.

Cocking is the bending of the hand backward or forward.

Hinging is the bending of the hand upward or downward. In a golf swing, the hinging action sets the club, not the cocking action.

When you swing your club to the top of your backswing, your wrist is hinged. During the downswing, as your hands drop to your hip level, your wrists must remain hinged. This is where most golfers straighten their wrists. The angle between your club shaft and your arm should remain perpendicular. The butt of your club should be pointing toward the target.

Visualize pulling the rope of a church-bell downward.

The farther you can keep this angle, the closer to impact is your release. Try doing this without a ball. Once you can hit your target on the ground consistently, place a ball there. You'll be able to see how lively the ball will travel.

COURSE MANAGEMENT

How to Handle Awkward Lies

Hills give the golf course a natural beauty. They also provide golfers with natural challenges to prove their mettle. The inclinations of a hill can pose problems. This is what can end up separating the men from the boys during a game.

For the big hitter, the problem is compounded because any error is magnified. Here are some scenarios you're likely to encounter on a hilly course:

Downhill - Ball Below Your Feet

This is a difficult lie. The ball will tend to go right so you can't swing aggressively.

Woods are out for this hole, unless you have a modern iron-wood with a high lofts. For irons, a 3-iron is the maximum club you can play.

Because of the nature of the lie, you may lose your balance if too much body action is involved. This is one area where you will have to play using arm-swing only. Therefore, take an extra club or two whenever possible.

Since the ball tends to fly right, you may expect a slice. Consequently, you aim left of the target. Play the ball forward in your stance, toward your left heel. Do NOT swing hard. Muscling of the ball will cause you to lose balance and mishit the ball.

Downhill - Ball Above Your Feet

There is a tendency for the ball to go left. However, you may end up hitting a thin shot and send the ball to the right. The nature of this lie encourages your body to slide downhill on the downswing.

Adopt a wider stance to reduce this slide. Play the ball toward the back and aim slightly to the right.

If you are using fairway woods, expect the ball to run a long way. If the slope is severe, use less club.

Uphill - Ball Below Your Feet

As long as the ball is below your feet, there's a tendency for your body to slide down. In order not to slide, you need to inhibit your body movement and rely on your arm swing only. However, you can be more aggressive in an uphill lie.

Slopes cancel each other out and you don't have to adjust for the shot going left or right. Just aim for a straight shot. Play the ball farther back in your stance to encourage a steeper contact.

Uphill – Ball Above Your Feet

This ball is going left. Of the four lies, this is the easiest one to handle.

The uphill adds loft and encourages the ball

to go high. Take one more club to counteract the loft and aim right. This will counteract the left-favored direction of the slope.

The slope may also make you fall back and loop the club around. Take the club straight back and swing along your body line. Drive through the ball with your body to avoid pulling it.

Red Flag

The red flag on the green means the hole is located at the front end of the green. For most golfers, the red flag spells trouble.

The reason is there's very little green to work with in front of the flag. Unlike a professional golfer, a high-handicapper usually can't produce enough backspin to make the ball move backwards. Thus, he has to resort to pitching or chipping the ball on the ground before the green.

Getting the ball close to the pin will depend a lot on the first bounce. This bounce will depend on where the ball lands.

Below are a few areas to watch:

Slopes

Very few greens are completely flat. You will see slopes leading to the green itself. The contour of the slope is important. If the slope is uphill, you know your ball will roll slower and stop quicker. Downhill is even trickier. You don't want to send the ball rolling past the hole for a three-putt. A slope to the right will send the ball to the right and vice versa.

High or Low Greens

If the green is located above you, your ball will land on a lower angle and roll faster. To stop it, you should play a high flop that drops down on a steep angle.

On the other hand, a green below you will deaden the momentum of the ball because of the higher angle of entry. To make sure your ball reaches the green, you may have to play a low running shot.

Grain

Grain is the direction the grass on the green is growing. It can be difficult to see from afar. Of course, you can always walk right up to the green to see the grain when you are chipping from less than 20 yards. If you see a shiny surface, you are looking at the back of grass blades that are pointing away from you. This means your ball will roll faster.

You can also determine the direction of the grain by the presence of water near the green. Grain will generally be pointing towards the water.

How to Play the Par 3

Don't mess around with a Par 3.

Nearly all golfers can reach this hole with one shot. Very few Par 3 holes exceed 180 yards. Surely you have a club that will reach that distance. Making a bogey is bad and a double bogey is a sin.

Play your shot carefully when facing a Par 3. Nine out of ten golfers will shoot short of the pin. Four out of ten will not reach the green altogether. So, take enough club to reach the flag. If the flag is 150 yards and your best shot for that yardage is a 6-iron, use a 5-iron.

Why?

How many times have you played your best shot?

Consider your starting tee. The distance should be shown on the board next to the tee box. Keep in mind that the distance is from middle of the tee to the middle of the green, not to the hole.

Also check out the flag position. You are shooting for the flag in a Par-3, not just the green. Look at the color of the flag. Red means in front. White means in the middle, and blue at the back. Depending on the size of the green, blue and red can mean one more club.

As you see, the flag observes the wind direction. Sometimes the wind direction at the tee box is different at the green. Wind at the green plays a greater importance than wind at the tee box.

Is the green higher than you?

If so, your ball will roll more as a result of a low angle of entry. If the green is lower, your ball will come to a faster stop.

Lastly, always use a tee. Tee the ball low so you can take a divot and create some backspin on the ball to let it stop faster.

Cold Weather Play

Ice, snow and chilling winds. All of these elements are just around the corner. It's time to put away your golf set and stay indoors. After Labor Day, the only hole golfers are interested in is the 19th.

Not for you. For a beginner, fall is the best time to play. Mother Nature is at her most splendid moment. Trees turn golden, the heat wave is gone, golf courses are not crowded, no more serious tournaments and the hustlers are gone. It's time to enjoy the scenery and play some relaxing golf.

You'll be surprised at how much better you play.

Since courses are relatively empty, you will probably be able to play alone.

This is the best opportunity for you to improve your short game skills. You know that you depend heavily on this part of the game. Now is the best time to hone these skills. Leave the big sticks in your closet.

Forget about taking a scorecard. Play target golf. Right from the tee-off, treat the fairway as a part of the green. Look for a particular spot and see if you can pitch your ball there. You can do this all the way to the green. Purposely pitch your ball into a bunker.

This is also the time for you to try out some variations. Instead of playing your usual high pitch on to the green, try the pitch and run. This is the time to add more skills to your arsenal. What you previously practiced on the driving range can be practiced right here on the course.

By the end of the round, you should find yourself getting nearer to your targets. You may even hit some directly!

On the green, you can polish your putting skills. No one will rush you. You can take your time reading the line. You can even move to another part of the green, drop a ball and then play. It will be like having nine different practice greens to practice. Playing nine holes is sufficient since you will spend longer at each hole.

You'll also have a great chance to practice in windy conditions. Use this opportunity to hone your wind playing skills.

You'll be wearing more clothing to keep your body warm in the open. This clothing can be a hindrance to your normal summer swing. If you insist on using that swing with all the clothing, your timing will suffer and you'll miss the sweet spot. The proper technique for the cold is to use a shorter backswing.

With the short backswing, your downswing will also be smooth and short. Your aim is to try and make solid contact. This technique applies to both your irons and your woods. The idea is to keep everything under control. When playing the irons, use a longer club to achieve the distance you normally get in summer.

Making a shorter swing doesn't mean swinging abruptly. Swing smooth and easy. Just take your backswing smoothly and stop when you feel the extra attire is in the way. That's the distance for your backswing. Let the word 'comfortable' be the guide to your play.

If you try swinging the way you did in summer with all your extra clothing, you'll create a bad swing. This can carry over and ruin your game when hot weather returns and all the extra clothing is gone.

On the other hand, keeping your swing smooth and short during winter will not hamper your game later on. Once summer arrives, your longer swing will come back naturally without all your cumbersome attire. In fact, your swing may even be smoother and more relaxed. This smooth and relaxed swing may be just what you need to propel that ball farther and more under control.

If you think you can use your normal swing by wearing less clothing, forget it. You need to be comfortably warm. If you develop a chill, your game will suffer. Long johns and corduroy slacks will be sufficient. For your upper body, wear several layers of lighter clothing instead of one thick garment. Wear a loose-fitting polyester windbreaker as your outer shell. Also use a scarf around your neck. Too warm is better than too cold. Top it off with a stocking cap. In extra cold weather, wear a ski band under your stocking cap to protect your ears. Make sure you also take a golf visor.

You need to be well equipped for the cold wind. Wear extra layers. Ordinary sweaters won't protect you adequately. Wear a nylon-type jacket as the top layer and wear long johns. It won't be any fun if the chill gets you. This is one case where more is better. You can always remove some clothing, but you can't add clothing you don't have.

Unfortunately, fall is followed by winter. But winter isn't barrier if weather permits. You need to make some adjustments for the winter.

1. Make sure your grips are in good condition, especially when wet. Clean your grips with a stiff brush and detergent. Swarfega is great for cleaning grips.

2. Make sure you wear or bring good waterproofs. Your shoes should also be waterproof. Wear all-weather gloves. You should also carry winter mitts, a nylon slip-on, a spare towel and a warm stocking cap.

Rough Play

As a beginner, you'll probably find your ball in the rough more often than on the fairway. Many golfers want to try for the green no matter what. Most of the time, they find themselves in worse trouble. You have to reconsider your game plan. You need to know how fast you can swing and the kind of a lie a ball is situated.

Don't be influenced by what you see on TV. The pros can make every rough shot look easy. They're not. The pros can generate tremendous swing speed to fly the ball out toward the green. If you can't swing fast enough, you'll require a more lofted club to get the ball out of the rough —a 9-iron or a pitching wedge. These clubs won't give you distance.

Let's take a look at the two kinds of lies:

Deep Lie

A deep lie is one where the ball is well inside the grass. When confronted with this situation, forget about getting the ball to travel far. Bringing the ball out on to the fairway should be your only goal.

Use the 9-iron or pitching wedge. Square the ball with the clubface. Your weight should be toward your left leg. Position the ball a little further back. This gives you a steeper entry angle.

To gain more control, hold the club further down the shaft. Use a three-quarter swing. Don't try to scoop the ball up like most beginners. Strike down aggressively. Keep a firm hold of the club to prevent the clubface from turning. You should also aim slightly to the right of the target because the grass will grab your heel and turn it left.

You don't have to swing hard. Use a smooth blow and keep your left hand moving down. Follow through as long as you can. Don't worry about that the grass may impede your club and ruin your follow-through. A good crisp chop will place the ball safely on to the fairway. Be sure you keep your eyes focused on the ball. Many beginners are so anxious to see where their ball is heading, they look up prematurely and mishit.

The Flier Lie

A flier lie is when the ball sits on top of the grass as if it's being teed up for you. As the name implies, the ball tends to travel farther than usual.

Consider yourself lucky to find such a lie, but don't get carried away. It may be trickier than you think. You have to hit this ball with a sweeping motion similar to the tee-off. This will cause the ball to travel farther.

You need to judge the distance cautiously. Not only will the ball travel farther, the blades of grass will get in between your ball and your clubface. This will cause your ball to jump off the clubface and result in less backspin on the ball. You should use one or two clubs less than usual.

This ball will reach the green and possibly beyond. Don't aim for the flag if it's located at a corner. Play into the middle of the green. Use a normal three-quarter swing. You may be tempted to swing if you take a club less.

Regardless of whether your ball is lying deep or sitting up, you should check if there is trouble ahead. You don't want to go from the frying pan into the fire. Play smart if there is a bunker or water ahead. Hit to a spot where you can make a good chip.

The 70 Per Cent Trick

You crack a huge swing at the ball on a long par-5 and watch it sailing out of bounds. You decide to play the next shot more conservatively and make a half swing. Though your ball remains in play, you don't like what you see. What's the matter? You swing hard and the ball goes haywire. You swing soft and the ball also goes haywire. How else can you swing?

You have to find your comfort zone. If anything beyond three-quarters of your full swing is uncontrollable, then you should stay below that limit. Similarly, if you cannot swing slower than 60%, don't go slower than that. Of course, we are talking about the full swing, and not chipping or pitching.

Make sure you are fully warmed up before this exercise. Once your muscles are loose and ready, make 10 full swings with your driver. Swing as hard as you possibly can without stopping. By the time you finish all ten swings, you will probably be breathless. Now you are ready.

Tee a ball up. Swing again but use only 70% of your previous swing. Since you are well within your comfort zone, you should be able to control this swing. You may be surprised to see how far the ball flies.

You may think you are using only 70%. Actually the percentage is probably closer to 85%. Your previous 10 hard swings are more than your full swing; they may be 120%. 70% of that will bring it to about 85% of your normal full swing. So you are really swinging at 85%. Since you are actually swinging at 70% and feeling comfortable, your ball is under better control.

Do you do this all the time? Not necessarily. As you proceed into the round, you may find your pace and tempo affected by surrounding situations. You may have to wait a long time for the group in front to move on. The sun may be getting hotter. You might get tired. All of these factors can upset your rhythm. You will start swinging harder and harder. This is the time you should use your hard practice swings. Relax and hit that ball 70%.

EQUIPMENT OVERVIEW

Enjoying the game of golf requires many kinds of skills. Sometimes a shot requires distance and sometimes accuracy. Some shots we hit from a tee, some we play from short grass and sometimes even from oh-so-dreaded places like rough, sand and dry dirt (hardpan). Each of such situations will benefits from a different club you use. Based on our abilities, some shots will be relatively easy and some will be a pain in the you-know-what.

Case in point: If the challenge is a 200 yard carry over water to a rather tight pin on a small green, the proper choice of club for a beginner, intermediate or advanced golfer will be different. The beginner will need all the help and forgiveness possible ("...*I swear, if I make this shot I'll be a good person for the rest of my life...*"). The intermediate may need a little less forgiveness but still wants to be comfortable with their club. The advanced player may want more subtle characteristics of feel and clubhead response that a beginner can't even imagine (... and still pledge to become a better person if the shot works out). In the past all three were left with only a few club choices, but - thankfully - today there are many more.

Which Clubs are most important?

As mentioned, golf requires several kinds of shots - drives, long approach shots, short approach shots, pitches, chips, sand shots, putts and a variety of (what family friendly books like ours) call trouble shots - they are called differently during play, though!

By far the most frequent shot is a putt. For an average golfer, the putter is used more than twice as much as any other club. Statistically, if a golfer shoots a score of 100, 35% - 40% of those strokes will be putts. So, quite obviously, the putter is the most important club you carry.

Generally, for most golfers the driver (also called the #1 wood) is used the next most often club, roughly on 14 out of 18 tee shots in average depending on ability level and course requirements. A good drive makes the rest of the shots on that hole easier. A lousy drive means, well, you know what... That makes the driver a very important club.

For players who have a hard time hitting the green in a regulation number of strokes, the wedges may be the second most used category of clubs. Even on a good day a beginner may spend a 15 to 20 strokes chipping up to the green.

The remaining challenges in a round will utilize the rest of the clubs in your set. It is likely that no one club will be used more than a few times. This means, in terms of club usage, the putter, driver and wedges are clearly used the most frequently while the rest of the clubs will bring up the rear.

Now let's look at the different clubs in more detail:

The Driver / 1 Wood

Take a look into the bag of any golfer. Chances are you'll see something in there with the word titanium on it. In recent years, the Periodic Table of Elements' 22nd element, Ti, has catapulted into the forefront as golf's most

precious metal. It's used in the manufacturing of putters, irons, and shafts-- even balls! However, nowhere is it more prevalent than in an oversized driver. Reason: it's very strong and very light. As a result, manufacturers are able to make oversize clubheads out of titanium and still maintain the same weight as a traditional size clubhead.

Titanium heads are usually 1/3 larger than most wooden or metal drivers or woods. Also, because titanium is lighter, manufacturers can make the shafts longer as well. In fact many titanium drivers are 2-3 inches longer than most other metal drivers. The result is simple. A bigger clubhead doesn't twist as much on off-center hits and a longer shaft translates into a bigger swing arc--both of these are key ingredients to added length off the tee.

Today's Driver Is Much Better

Years ago, golfers played with persimmon and laminated woods. In truth, when these clubs were struck properly, nothing felt better. However, there are only so many Tiger Woods out there and these clubs were anything but forgiving on mis-hits. When you hit today's oversized titanium driver off the heel or toe, you still come away with a salvageable shot. Since most golfers miss more often than they hit the ball perfectly, the larger titanium heads have big advantages. They make the ball go a greater distance on off-center hits. So with titanium, it's not that the material itself that makes the ball go farther, it's that the bigger head makes your misses go farther. When your grandfather mis-hit his persimmon club, he could lose 50 yards of distance. In that sense, titanium and oversized-head technology has made the average player better. It has also allowed senior players to keep up with the youngsters off the tee. Titanium and other metal drivers are also more durable than wooden woods.

The High Cost of Titanium

Titanium is the fourth most available element in the world. It's found in beach sand throughout the world, especially in Australia and China. Despite this abundance, Ti drivers are more expensive than steel models. That's because it's very difficult to manufacture a titanium head. Mining titanium from beach sand is not an easy process. As a result, the raw material cost is higher than steel. Secondly, titanium must be cast in a vacuum, a chamber without air. Even if done properly, this is expensive, because many clubheads don't come out perfect and must be destroyed. The shaft is also a factor. Most titanium woods are made using very lightweight graphite shafts. The lighter the shaft, the harder they are to make and the more expensive they become. Of course, some of titanium's high price is the result of marketing and advertising costs.

Titanium Might Suit You

Initially, these drivers were developed to help the average player or short hitter get added distance off the tee. For this type of player, titanium is ideal. However, even professionals have benefited from titanium. Today's tour players who would have had below-average length 15 years ago are now keeping up with their playing partners.

Pick the Right Loft for You

When you're spending hard-earned money on a product, make sure that it perfectly fits your game. Don't automatically purchase a driver with the stiffest shaft or lowest loft. Make sure you understand your game. Remember, the greater the loft, the easier it will be to control. A higher lofted club gives you more carry but less roll, and vice versa. It's important to note that a titanium driver hits the ball higher than you might expect. This is due to the center of gravity being farther back in the clubhead and the shaft being longer. Many times a 9-degree titanium driver will produce the same ball flight as a 10.5-degree stainless metal wood. Because titanium clubs are longer, it's important to choose a club that gives you the best combination of accuracy and distance. Distance is useless without accuracy. Remember, the longer the shaft, the more difficult any club is to control. As a beginner you should select a driver with a deeper face to promote added role and a more controllable, boring trajectory--all important to added length off the tee. However, if you already hit a low ball, take this into account. For example, select a deep-face driver with   a   higher   loft

Choose the Right Shaft

The most important component of any golf club is the shaft. In a nutshell, steel gives you more accuracy than graphite. Graphite shafts give you more distance. That's because steel flexes less than graphite at impact. The only time this isn't true is when manufacturers add material into the graphite (boron, etc.) to make it flex less or perform more like steel. Graphite is ideal for woman and senior players for many reasons. It's lighter, absorbs the shock of impact better, and generally has a lower flex point to help you get the ball airborne. Because it's lighter, it's also better for those players experiencing back problems. A titanium head combined with a steel shaft is for the golfer who has plenty of strength but wants more forgiveness on mis-hits.

One Final Note: It's More the Golfer than the Club

Your titanium driver will help you hit the ball farther - especially on off-center hits. However, it is not a cure-all. It is important to always dedicate sufficient time to practicing your swing and fundamentals.

Fairway Woods

The second shot on a par-5 has been called the most boring shot in golf. Yet, the club that most players use for that shot, makes most players face two challenges with this shot: to hit it farther and to hit it straighter. Outside of working to make your golf swing more effective, which you should be doing, the fairway wood can help to solve the farther/straighter problem. It can probably also save you a couple of strokes.

The New Era

There was a time when woods were made out of...wood. In fact, these were the clubs of choice during the feathery-ball era, which – as described earlier - lasted from the 15th Century to the middle of the 19th Century. With the introduction of the Taylor Made Pittsburgh Persimmon metal-headed driver in 1979, golf club design changed again. Although this club wasn't immediately embraced by purists because of its sound at impact and nontraditional appearance, it nonetheless allowed club designers greater latitude.

With metal (usually steel), the designer can easily make the clubhead larger or smaller, add runners to the sole, or build out the toe--all in an effort to make the club perform better. This helps you to hit the ball straighter and with more confidence. Steel also has a higher strength-to-weight ratio than wood, allowing the club maker to use less material without sacrificing strength. The result is a lighter, easier-to-swing clubhead. Even more, to help the club perform better and be more forgiving, weight is moved to the perimeter of the clubhead to help it square at impact and be more stable on off-center hits.

Your Best Friend

The Fairway Wood can make your wandering tee shot a little less problematic and the long par-4s a little more reachable. And other than the short irons, the fairway woods are the easiest clubs to hit. Most mid-to-high-handicap players have much more confidence in a fairway wood than either their driver or a long iron.

The ease in hitting is accomplished by two design features. The larger clubhead, when compared to an iron, provides greater stability because it is less likely to twist through impact. This helps you return the clubface to square at impact and produces straighter ball flight.

The loft of a fairway wood is typically 15 degrees for a standard 3-wood, 19 degrees for a 5-wood, and 24 degrees for a 7-wood. The loft of the 5-wood corresponds to a 2-iron, and the 7-wood to a 4-iron. Many intermediate golfers are using these woods as reliable substitutes for the corresponding irons.

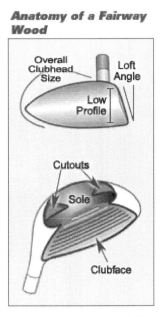

Here are some of the technical advances you can expect to find in this new generation of metalwoods:

• Low center of gravity

Because a metalwood is hollow, the weight is concentrated to the sole and the outside of the clubhead to help get the ball airborne and increase the sweetspot.

• Stronger lofts

The low center of gravity means the manufacturer can use stronger lofts without compromising trajectory. This translates to added distance.

• Miracle metals

In the last few years, new-age steels and titanium have been used to provide even more advantages. These light, strong materials allow the club designer to maintain the strength and integrity of the clubhead and place yet more weight on the sole, the back, the heel, and the toe for greater stability through impact.

• Inserts

A change of rules in '92 allowed for inserts in metal clubs (irons and woods). For instance, some clubs now have forged steel inserts in the face. This harder-hitting surface provides greater impact force and a better "feel" for the player. A complaint among better players was that metalwoods didn't provide response on off-center hits. The insert helps to combine the advantages of a perimeter-weighted metalwood with the more traditional response at impact.

• Trouble clubs

Many fairway woods are designed as trouble clubs. Instead of a flat sole, these clubs have a rounded or convex sole, and some employ cutouts or bulges to ensure better contact in the rough or from fairway bunkers. This can prove as invaluable to scoring well as any club in the bag.

Irons

Having a good Set of Irons that you can trust is very comforting. Sure, driving the ball is fun, but in a round of golf it's the irons you count on to get you on the green and in position to do well. The good news is that modern technology has made irons easier to hit than ever. This section will help you learn the basics of iron design, how they've improved, and which clubs are best suited for your game.

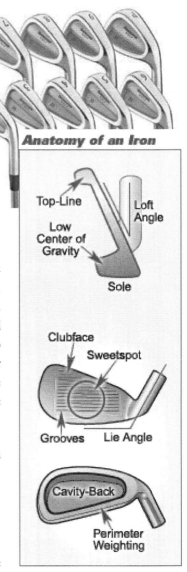

Anatomy of an Iron

Most iron sets consist of a 3-iron through pitching wedge (listed as 3-PW). This accounts for 8 of the 14 clubs you can carry according to the Rules of Golf, leaving room for a putter and three woods. Some players substitute a high-lofted wood for the 3-iron because they find it easier to hit. This is a good strategy. However, stronger players who don't have a problem getting the ball up may still prefer to use the more accurate long irons.

Here's a guide to the key features of today's irons:

• **Blade versus cavity-back**

A blade iron offers a smaller hitting surface and a thin top-line (portion of the clubhead viewed at address). It also has more mass behind the middle of the clubhead, sometimes called a "muscle-back," that gives a very soft feeling when hit properly. In contrast, a cavity-back or perimeter-weighted club has more weight around the outside edges of the clubhead to produce a larger sweetspot. The easiest-hitting irons of all generally have a large cavity-back, thick top-line, and oversize clubface. But increasingly, clubmakers are offering designs that incorporate the forgiving benefits of cavity-back in a blade style with a thinner top-line. For many traditionalist golfers, this is the answer.

• Casting versus forging

Up until the early 1970s, forged steel clubheads accounted for more than 90% of all irons made. This model involves hammering and shaping the clubhead. Now, investment casting has taken over as the primary manufacturing method. Casting, in which the metal is poured into a mold, costs less and makes it easier to produce the complex shapes of today's perimeter-weighted, cavity-back designs within tight specifications. However, forging is not likely to disappear because many golfers believe it offers better feel and ball "workability." It also offers a cleaner look for the tradition-minded golfer.

• Hosel offset

This is measured from the leading edge of the hosel (where the shaft enters the clubhead) to the farthest front portion of the clubface. Why is it important? A club with offset contacts the ball later than a club without offset. This helps "square" the clubface at impact and reduces the tendency to slice (ball going right for right-handed golfers).

• Progressive weighting

This involves placing a heavier material, such as copper or tungsten, in the sole of lower-lofted irons. This helps lower the center of gravity and get the ball in the air. Progressive weighting is generally eliminated in the shorter irons to help produce a lower, flatter trajectory.

• *Grooves or scoring lines*

Grooves add spin and control to the ball's flight. An iron with no grooves causes the ball to "squirt" off the face. Backspin may decrease distance slightly but greatly enhances control. Karsten Solheim, legendary founder of Ping, brought attention to the value of grooves when players of his clubs with larger, sharper grooves began showing superior control--especially out of rough lies. The USGA strictly controls the depth and distance between scoring lines on the clubface to ensure fairness.

• *Lie*

This is the angle of the sole (bottom) of the club as it relates to the shaft. Too "flat" a lie places the heel of the club in the air, while too upright a lie angle causes the toe to be in the air at address. Lie angle for all custom clubs should be tailored to your body.

• *Loft*

This is the clubface angle relative to the shaft, and determines the trajectory of your shots. It varies from about 22 degrees in a 3-iron for a lower, longer trajectory to 64 degrees in a wedge for short, high shots.

• *Satin finish vs. polish or chrome*

This is merely a cosmetic question. A satin finish can be very attractive, but in general has a duller appearance than polished or chrome-finish clubheads.

• *Sole*

This is the very bottom part of the clubhead. If you look closely at the sole of your club, you'll notice it has a slight curvature from toe to heel and from leading edge to trailing edge. This "camber" or "radius sole" makes it easier to hit consistent shots. Sole width is another factor. A narrower sole works better from fairway and tight lie conditions while a wider sole is better for plush lies.

Wedges

Wedges have come a long way in recent years. New lofts and clubhead shapes have prompted many players to carry as many as four wedges, for every conceivable situation around the green. If you're just carrying the old reliable pitching wedge, you're missing out on some simple ways to lower your scores. After all, more than 70% of your game is played from 100 yards or closer.

How Wedges Work

All wedges are characterized by high lofts (typically 45-60 degrees) to increase trajectory, and significant sole weighting to help you penetrate sand or grass. Most are also heavier overall. But that's where the similarities end. Each wedge type has its own characteristics, making it suited to a particular distance or lie.

One important characteristic is the bounce angle. As the name implies, this feature enables the clubhead to "bounce" out of the sand or rough without digging in. If you look at the sole of a sand wedge, for instance, you'll notice that the trailing edge hangs below the leading edge. Bounce is the angle formed by the leading edge and the ground. This tiny angle (maximum 16 degrees) doesn't sound like

Anatomy of a Wedge

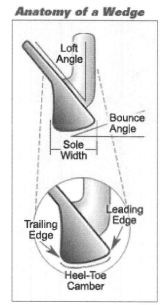

much, but it's what makes it worthwhile for you to carry a good sand wedge in your bag. Without bounce, you may just stay in that bunker forever. And in

191

general, less experienced players should use a club with more bounce in soft or fluffy lies.

As with putters, wedges are the focus of a lot of experimentation in materials and **face inserts**. Clubheads are often made of softer materials, such as copper or beryllium alloy, to increase feel and touch around the green. Some are intended to rust over time, giving a unique appearance. Manufacturers have also devised unique ways to impart precise spin on the ball and help it hold the green upon landing. The most basic treatment is scoring or sandblasting of the face. U-shaped grooves, which are square at the bottom, are also used. Still another method is to use a different material altogether in the face, such as a super-hard diamond compound.

One major development has been the introduction of the "gap" or "dual" wedge. As manufacturers decreased the loft of the typical pitching wedge to increase its distance (a little sleight of hand), they created a "gap" between it and the next longest club, the sand wedge (see graphic below). Thus, in order of distance, the progression is as follows: pitching wedge, gap wedge, sand wedge, and lob wedge. They are described here in order.

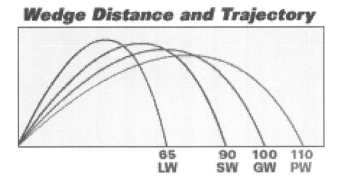

Pitching Wedge

This club has typically 45-49 degrees of loft and is used for longer approach shots (about 110 yards for men, 90 yards for women). Because it's most often hit from the grass, it has minimal bounce (2-5 degrees). In fact, a lot of bounce would be undesirable in this club, because it would make it more difficult to get the leading edge under the ball, causing you to skull it.

Gap Wedge

This club has typically 49-54 degrees of loft and is used for shots of about 100 yards for men, or about 95 yards for women. Bounce is typically 5-12 degrees. But don't pick a gap wedge at random. Choose a loft that divides the "gap" evenly between your pitching and sand wedges. For instance, if you have a 48-degree PW and a 56-degree SW, buy a gap wedge with 52 degrees. This club is also known as a "dual" or "attack" wedge.

Sand Wedge

This club has typically 54-57 degrees of loft and is used for shots of about 90 yards maximum for men, or about 80 yards for women. It also has the most unique clubhead of the bunch, with lots of bounce (10-16 degrees) and another feature called **heel-toe camber**. This is what gives the sand wedge an oval shape on the bottom of the face. Finally, sand wedges have more **sole width** (the distance between the leading and trailing edge). All these features are designed to reduce the risk of digging in.

Lob Wedge

This club has 57 or more degrees of loft and is used for shots of about 65 yards maximum for men, or 60 yards for women. These clubs, also called "finesse" wedges, are for "touch" shots around the green that need to get into the air quickly and land softly. Bounce is minimal (0-10 degrees), because in these situations there is generally very little room under the ball, and a tiny error can make the club bounce off the ground and cause a skulled shot. It has less sole width and a sharp leading edge. One reason many players like this club is because it allows a full, unimpeded swing to cover a short distance, rather than making you rely on an abbreviated swing. The ball flies short and high.

Hybrid Clubs

If you follow golf on television or subscribe to golf magazines then you have likely witnessed the mounting discussion surrounding Hybrid (sometimes referred to as utility) clubs. The buzz is starting to spread, and you are starting to hear more about hybrids because they are becoming the hottest and most popular club to carry in your bag. Unlike some clubs that are specifically designed for certain players or skill levels, hybrids are suited for both, recreational players and touring pros.

The word hybrid means something that is of mixed origin or composition. In golf, they have taken ideologies of both a wood and iron design and combined them, to manufacture some of the most forgiving and easiest clubs to hit to date. Features you will find on the hybrid are:

- Flatness of the face on the hybrid wood. Woods have a curve on the face but the hybrids are flat just like an iron.

- Weighting that is distributed throughout the club like an iron or fairway wood. Most woods have the focus of the weight distributed towards the front.

- A wide sole like a fairway wood, with a club length similar to an iron rather than a wood.

The main idea behind the hybrid wood is to be interchangeable and utilize the characteristics of both an iron and a wood. The resultant club is typically easier to hit with less effort than a traditional long and lower lofted iron. The term "long iron" normally describes all the clubs from a two iron through five.

There are multiple reasons why many recreational golfers struggle with long iron shots and the goal of the hybrid wood is to make it easier for you. The most common problems are:

- Not being able to make a complete shoulder turn on the backswing.

- Swinging too hard and throwing off tempo.

- Lower lofted clubs are harder to hit.

The elite players who do all the right things with long irons save strokes during the average round, but the majority of players struggle with them, and now have an alternative in the hybrid club. The long narrow face and a wide sole of hybrid clubs utilizes a low center of gravity cog, which helps players with slower swing speeds launch the ball with little effort, making a hybrid club similar to playing a wood in that it lends itself to the sweeping style swing rather than picking the ball off the turf with greater effort as a traditional iron. Effectively, all players benefit, but particularly grateful are those players who have lost swing speed due to age, injury or other physically conditions that have prevented them from making a full shoulder turn on the backswing. Hybrids allow for a shorter back swing while launching the same distance you are use to experiencing with a wood.

The face of a hybrid is manufactured out of harder 17-4 stainless steel, similar to a fairway wood, which helps with the ball compression and forgiveness of the club. The hardness of the metal allows a slower swing speed to produce distance that you would normally see with a faster swing speed. Not only will you see longer distances from the hybrid wood, you should see more accuracy because the hybrid allows for a greater margin for error. All this from a club that is shorter and lighter than its performance-matching counterparts.

Many players using Hybrids are not only replacing long irons but are using them as fairway woods as well. Some of the loft angles on Hybrid clubs match those of a 3 and 5 wood but are shorter, lighter and more versatile.

Hybrids are extremely versatile and can be used easily from the fairway, rough or tee, and they are a great stroke saver. If you suffer, as many do, from the long iron blues, you should consider a hybrid to compliment your game. Again I recommend to check out www.GolfBargainShop.com for their selection and great prices.

Putters

The Putter is one piece of equipment with which you can truly express yourself. Beside a colorful shirt or a jaunty cap, the putter best matches the person because the putter must match the player's putting style.

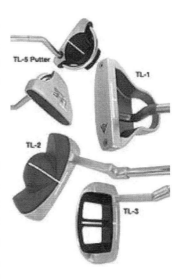

Mostly, this is due to "feel": an elusive quality that's nearly impossible to describe, yet most golfers understand it. Feel doesn't just mean how the putter physically feels to the touch or when stroking a putt. It's the response you gets when holding the putter, taking a practice stroke, drawing the putter back, and making contact with the ball. Feel takes the putting stroke and transforms the act from science to art. For sure, much of this takes place between the ears. But the right Putter can certainly help. Head materials, head designs, and grips are just a few of the tools club makers use to achieve the right feel.

Head Shape

The greatest variations in putter design are in the head itself. From blade, to mallet, to oversize, the putter head has included all things great and small. The blade appears thin when you look down from the top, and it has no material behind it. A traditional blade putter head is about the thickness of your finger. This type of putter is less forgiving

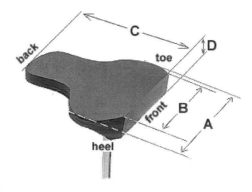

on off-center hits, but provides accuracy. Many blades now retain a thin top

197

line appearance, but have material on the back of the putter head that's been hollowed out in a cavity-back design to reduce twisting at contact.

A mallet is larger and wider than a blade, often having a broad surface that contacts the ground.

Some models include alignment lines to assist in lining up a putt. They can be as simple as a notch in the center of the top line of the putter, or as elaborate as a system of lines and arrows pointing in the direction that you'll be hitting the ball. Some people find them distracting, but these lines used in conjunction with the trademark on the ball can aid putts tremendously.

Head Materials

Most putter heads are made of stainless or carbon steel. Bronze and brass are also used, and provide a softer feel. Aluminum is also used for a soft feel and lightweight. Graphite, polymers and other plastics are used to make a putter head that is very resilient and very light. These materials generally make the head more expensive.

Inserts

Putter heads have been the focus of a lot of experimentation in materials. Some have lightweight composite inserts in the face, which, by ratio, places more weight in the toe and heel. Inserts are a relatively new design element in putters. They're intended to provide greater response at contact. Most inserts are a synthetic material; although, some are a softer metal such as aluminum. Some companies have experimented with rubber faces, aluminum honeycomb-like structures, and the like. The insert conforms to the ball on contact and generates a softer feel through the shaft and to your hands. The result is a more controlled roll. Sometimes, the face of metal putter heads are milled--material is cut away to achieve an extremely flat surface and maximized feel.

Weight

Weight is the greatest contributor to how the putter feels in your hands. You notice it the moment you pick it up. A putter head that is too light contributes to a "handsy" putting style where the hands control the stroke, making the putter head pass through the contact zone too quickly. This usually causes putts to run long. A heavy putter head creates drag in the stroke. The putter head passes through the contact zone too slowly, causing putts to come up short.

In general, a mallet putter is somewhat heavier. Steel putter heads are lighter than bronze, brass, or aluminum models. Overall, it's better to err on the side of a lighter putter. A heavier putter is less consistent for you over the course of 18 holes.

Balance

When a putter head is balanced, it resists twisting at impact, which helps impart a more consistent roll to the ball. To test this, balance a putter on your finger by placing your finger under the shaft near the putter head. With a face-balanced putter, the clubface remains nearly parallel to the ground. A face-balanced putter can be achieved through a cavity-back design, where more weight is placed in the heel and toe.

Length

Length should be determined by your putting stance. The more you crouch over the ball, the shorter the putter needs to be. The more you stand up, the longer the putter should be. Most putters are 34 or 35 inches long. Try one of each. Keep in mind that a longer putter is more difficult to control and may not impart as much feel.

Loft

As much as it appears that the face of a putter is straight up and down, there is a slight degree of loft on every putter--usually about four degrees. Loft helps the ball to roll properly. On the putting stroke, the ball is actually lifted slightly at impact, skids a bit due to backspin, and then begins to roll over and toward the target.

Shafts

Putters can either be center shafted (the shaft connects near the middle of the putter head) or heel shafted (the shaft connects near the heel). An offset shaft helps set up a proper stroke. In this design, a bend in the hosel (where the shaft enters the clubhead) or shaft helps keep your hands ahead of the ball, promoting a smoother stroke. Shafts can also be in hosel (the hosel surrounds the shaft) or over hosel (the shaft surround the hosel). With some models, there is no hosel. These are mostly aesthetic concerns.

Grips

Grips are different, too. Most putter grips are larger than those on your other clubs. This helps promote a lighter grip pressure and prevents the wrists from breaking too easily.

GOLF BALLS

Golf's biggest advancements have come via dramatic improvements in ball construction. Compared to 30 years ago, today's golf ball travels farther, rolls longer, doesn't lose its round, flies straighter, and won't split its cover if you look at it wrong. Precisely engineered dimple patterns have allowed manufacturers to alter everything from trajectory to spin rates. As a result of these breakthroughs, players now have the opportunity to choose and play the best ball for their games.

Years ago, everyone played with a soft, easy-cutting, natural rubber, balata-covered ball--whether you were a scratch player or a 25 handicap. Today, you're lucky to have numerous choices. However, options don't necessarily make things easier. In fact, finding the right ball for your game can be confusing. Rather than have you spend hours researching your options, we did it for you.

Development of the Golf Ball

The first golfers of Scotland played with balls made of hardwood. In 1618, a ball called a "featherie" was introduced. Goose feathers were wrapped in leather and both the leather and feathers were soaked to make the ball harder.

In 1849, Rev Adam Paterson introduced a ball called the "guttie" made from the sap of the gutta tree. The guttie was virtually indestructible and much cheaper to produce than the "featherie". Unfortunately, the ball couldn't travel far and golfers had trouble hitting it out of the rough.

With industrialization, companies began producing rubber balls from molds. In 1898, Coburn Haskell obtained a patent for a golf ball made of rubberized thread wrapped around a solid rubber core in a gutta-percha casing. This ball was much easier to hit and control. Consequently, golf's popularity in the US increased.

Eventually, the gutta-percha covered cover was replaced with gutta-balata. Gutta-balata is a hard rubber-like material made by drying the milky juice of the bully tree found in the West Indies. Balata is tough, inelastic and water-resistant. Therefore, the balata ball became the ball of choice for most golfers.

In the late 1950s, a chemist named Richard Rees invented a resin material called Surlyn. This material became the staple skin of the majority of wound golf balls on the market. At about the same time, Robert Molitor, a chemical engineer with Spalding, invented the two-piece golf ball. Although these balls were very tough and could travel a great distance, they were very hard. Researchers used terpolymers to soften the balls which give golfers a better feel.

Then came the Dimples...

Initially golf balls were smooth spheres. Then in 1908, William Taylor introduced dimples to the Haskell ball. This proved the most successful aerodynamic pattern ever and is still used today.

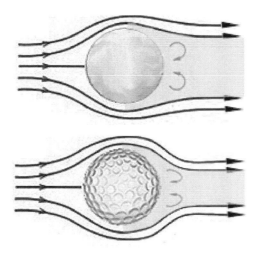

Aerodynamic physics show that when a spherical object travels through fluid, air or water, it separates the fluid leaving an area behind that slows it down. This area, called the drag, slows down the motion of the object considerably.

There are two kinds of flow: laminar and turbulent.

In a smooth sphere, laminar flow exists. Laminar flow is when the fluid separates from the object immediately after passing through it. This results in an initial area of drag behind the object that is almost as wide as the object's circumference.

Roughness in an object's surface, such as the dimples in a golf ball, changes the flow from laminar to turbulent. In a turbulent flow, the fluid clings on to the object longer before separating. This forms a smaller initial area behind the object which enables the object to travel farther.

When a golf ball spins backwards, the attached air at the back of the ball is pushed downwards. This helps to lift the ball. Therefore, the dimples not only help the ball to travel farther, they also help it to travel higher into the air.

The number, size and shape of the dimples can influence the flight of a ball. Companies are still researching these factors.

Golf Ball Specifics

In order to provide a fair game, the golf ball must be standardized. This standard is set by the United States Golf Association (USGA) for the United States and Mexico, and the R&A (taken from the Royal and Ancient Golf Club of St Andrews) for the rest of the world.

Each golf ball must pass the following requirements to be considered legal:

- **Weight** – The golf ball must not weigh more than 1.620 ounces (45.93gm). There is no minimum weight.

- **Size** – The diameter of the golf ball must not be smaller than 1.680 inches (42.67mm). There is no maximum size.

- **Spherical Symmetry** – The golf ball must be symmetrical in shape.

- **Initial Velocity** – The golf ball must not exceed a certain initial takeoff speed.

- **Overall Distance Standard** – The golf ball must not exceed a certain overall distance, including roll.

Golf Ball Numbers

Most golfers just look at the name brand of the golf ball they're using. They only look at a golf ball's number when attempting to identify it from another.

However, the numbers exist for more than mere identification:

- **Single-Digit** – A single digit on a golf ball is mainly used for identification purposes. The numbers generally range from 1 to 4.

- **70-200** – A number ranging from 70-200 indicates the compression rating. Compression relates to the hardness of a golf ball. The higher the number, the harder the ball (please see below for more on compression). The most common compression range is 90 to 100. Unfortunately, this number is not standardized.

- **300-400** – A ball with a number ranging from 300 to 400 indicates the number of dimples on the ball.

The golf ball underwent a dramatic change in recent years. In 1996, the multilayered ball was created to assist golfers striving for more distance. The Top-Flite Strata was the first multilayer ball to be produced. This ball introduced a hard mantle to bridge the gap between the solid core and the cover. This so-called mantle helps to reduce the spin created by the driver. According to the manufacturer, this reduces the height and increases the distance.

At turn of the century, another distance ball was born. The Titleist Pro V1 featured a solid core and polyurethane cover. According to Golf Digest, this ball outdistanced the others by more than 6 yards.

Every golfer's dream is to hit the ball farther and farther. In order to do so, golfers seek the highest quality of balls on the market.

The current top of the line balls require a high level of skill to achieve the desired distance. Unfortunately, most golfers who purchase these balls don't have the necessary skill. The quest carries on as golf ball manufacturers continue to push the envelope.

Ball Types

There are two main classes of balls: spin, and distance.

Spin: Designed to spin more. Often, they are of three-piece construction. A central core (liquid in the highest spin balls) is surrounded by rubber windings, which is often covered with a thin, soft material called balata. These balls spin more, making them easier to draw or fade, and they hold the green. They also have a softer feel but won't travel as far as distance balls. Less expensive versions of these balls offer a measure of durability. Their cover is typically Surlyn (a durable, synthetic material) or a Surlyn blend, they may be two-piece rather than three-piece, and have a solid core.

Distance: Made with harder, more-durable covers and solid cores. Most are two piece. The inside of the distance ball is a firm synthetic material. The combined firmness of the cover and core allow the ball to travel longer distances and be very durable. However, these balls don't spin a great amount. Less spin means less control and stopping ability in certain cases. These have a harder feel than balls with wound construction.

Covers: Balata vs. Surlyn

Balata and Surlyn are popular ball-covering materials. However, there are typically other differences between balata and surlyn balls besides just the cover:

Surlyn

A surlyn covered ball is typically a two-piece ball: a solid core with the surlyn cover. Surlyn is a man made "uncuttable" substance which is designed to eliminate the cuts and nicks. The drawbacks of the harder ball are that it is more difficult to "shape" his/her shot *(fade/draw)*, and get "action" *(backspin)* on the greens.

Balata

A balata covered ball is typically a three-piece ball: a core wound with rubber and covered with balata. There has been a lot of discussion as to what "balata" is. Let's just say that balata is a soft substance which leads to cuts and nicks. This "softness" is said to offer "better playability" which is to say that the golfer can "shape" his/her shot *(fade/draw)*, and get more "action" *(backspin)* on the greens.

Compression

Golf ball manufacturers use compression machines to measure how much their balls will deform under a certain weight. If a ball doesn't deform, it's given a 200 compression rating. The amount of deformation, measured in thousandths of an inch is read for a ball that deforms. This number is multiplied by 1000 and then subtracted from 200. Therefore, if a the ball measures only 1.575 inches instead of the original 1.680 inches, the amount of deformation is $1.680 - 1.575 = 0.105$.

Multiplying this number by 1000 yields 105, and subtracting 105 from 200 gives 95 as the compression rate of the ball.

The lower the compression rate, the more the ball can be compressed. This produces a softer the ball that will give the player more feel. Unfortunately, not all machines used to measure compression are equal. Consequently, different manufacturers may indicate different numbers for the same ball. The compression rate may also be shown on a ball.

Golfers with average swing speeds should use Compression 100. Golfers with low swing speeds as well as ladies and seniors, should use Compression 80. Temperature also affects the performance of the ball. Warm temperature has a positive effect on high compression balls, whereas cool temperature has the same effect on low compression balls.

Armed with this knowledge, you may feel ready to choose your ball. However, you need to learn what balls are specially made for first:

- **Distance** – A 'distance' ball is constructed to fly farther without much deviation from the intended path. This is beneficial; it can mean the difference between your ball lying on the fairway, in the rough or even in a hazard. The downside of a 'distance' ball is its inability to stop quickly. Approach shots to the green must be played with more caution when using a 'distance' ball.

- **Spin** – A 'spin' ball is constructed with more spin in mind. The cover of this ball is softer so more spin is imparted when struck. A draw curves more to the left and a fade more to the right. More backspin is also imparted. This makes it a great ball to play into the green where it needs to stop quickly.

- **Control** – A 'control' ball is a 'distance' ball that is constructed to stop quickly on the green. It is better behaved than the "spin" ball. You may wonder how a ball can do such amazing things. The Nike One and the Titleist ProV1 are two such balls already on the market.

- **Lady** – A 'lady' or 'senior' ball is designed for golfers with slower swings.

Putting

All balls behave differently. This behavior is apparent on the putting green. Harder balls roll farther than softer balls. The difference in distance may surprise you. Professional instructors always advise their students to putt with the same type of ball. This will enable beginners to develop feel and calibrate the distance of their putting strokes.

No golf ball is perfect. In fact, most balls aren't well balanced and don't always roll the same way during a putt. Next time you miss a 4-foot putt, blame it on the ball. Premium balls are subject to higher quality control and less likely to drift.

Budget

At the end of the day, your choice boils down to budget. It's bad practice to play with premium balls until each one is scratched and out of shape. It is much better to play with a cheaper ball that you can replace regularly.

Furthermore, in case you intend to participate in a club competition, you are better off playing with your usual cheap balls than buying new premium balls. Although your usual balls may not look good, you know how they'll behave.

What We Recommend

Most novice players should try balls that use a more durable cover so that mis-hits don't ruin the ball's roundness and flight characteristics. Advanced players should try to stay away from Surlyn covered two-piece balls, which don't offer as much feel and lack the ability to "work" the ball. Try a few different balls in the appropriate category for you and find one that makes you feel lucky. Confidence is half the battle! Here are some pointers:

Determine which compression is best for you.

Compression is a measure of how hard the ball may feel--the higher the compression number the harder the feel (and the less it compresses during impact). A common misconception among players is that a 100-compression ball always flies farther. This is not true. Clubhead speed, rather than compression, is most important to distance. For some golfers, a lower-compression ball will fly farther.

Determine if you like two- or three-piece balls.

Today, spin rates are a function of cover softness rather than construction. Still, a two-piece ball generally produces more distance and less spin, while a three-piece ball gives you more feel and additional spin. A three-piece ball often flies higher as well, because spin is what causes a golf ball to lift.

Pick a ball that suits your level of play.

If you mishit or top the ball a lot, you're not going to want an easy-cutting balata-covered ball. Conversely, if you're a scratch player, you're not going to want something that feels hard and gives you less spin and control--even if it won't cut.

Choose a ball that fits your budget.

Golf is an expensive sport. Some balls cost more than $3 a piece. Find the right ball for your budget. Often similar balls--of the same construction--vary greatly in price. Be conscious of this. Generally, balata-covered balls cost more, while the Surlyn covered balls cost less.

Consider the material.

While most two-piece balls have a synthetic core that varies only in softness, some companies are now adding exotic materials such as tungsten and titanium. Companies claim that because these exotic materials are dense and the center of gravity is more centrally located, the balls spin more. Some companies use these materials in ball covers, promising added feel and distance. Other companies use multilayer construction. These are higher-priced balls generally made with synthetic covers. They provide a good combination of durability, soft feel, and consistency.

PURCHASING GOLF EQUIPMENT – WHAT TO LOOK OUT FOR

We all want to improve our game-whether you're a beginner, an intermediate, or a highly skilled player. The better you are, the more you enjoy playing. While practice is the key to improving, other factors sometimes impede your progress, like your clubs. Having the right clubs increases your chance of playing well and instills self-confidence-a critical factor in improving your game.

But finding the right clubs is a challenge. With so many options out there, it's hard to know which ones are right for you. Our buyers guide provides information that will help you choose the right clubs for you. Easy to understand, the guide offers a step-by-step approach for selecting the right clubs.

When it comes to buying equipment, we all think alike: The higher the price, the better the clubs. While price often indicates quality, those expensive brand name clubs touted by a PGA pro may not be right for you. You don't need a $1200 set of clubs to play well. In fact, you can play better with clubs costing hundreds less than brand names if they fit your swing and your game. How do you find the right clubs?

Knowledge is the key to selecting your clubs. Knowing how a club affects your swing and your ball striking helps you choose a set that's right for you. That's something only you can do. Your favourite salesman at the local pro shop-as knowledgeable as he is about clubs-can provide some help, but it's limited, since he probably doesn't know how you play. Using our guide will help you make a better, more informed decision.

The major components of a golf club are the head, the shaft, and the grip. These components come in a variety of makes, models, sizes, and materials. If one of these components doesn't match your swing or if your clubs are too old, you'll struggle to improve your game. Below are details on these key components.

Club Head

Manufacturers have come a long way in club making technology. Today, clubs are more forgiving than ever, and nowhere is the impact of those advances felt more than in club head design and construction. A club head's main characteristics are offset, perimeter weighting, sole width, heel-to-toe length, and face height.

Offset

Offset is the amount the face of a club sits back from the hosel of the club. Offset reduces the chances of hitting a slice and increases the chances making solid contact with the ball. Solid contact affects distance and accuracy. Better golfers require less offset than poorer players. In fact,

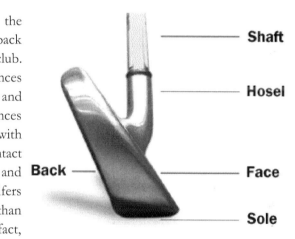

offset can be a major factor in helping players with high handicaps play well. Even players with lower handicaps benefit from using clubs with offset club heads.

Perimeter Weighting

Perimeter weighting places more material around the club head's perimeter than its center, creating a larger sweet spot on the club. This design makes the club more forgiving when hit and reduces the effects of miss-hits. Better players prefer the club head's mass behind the center to achieve more distance. Poorer players want the weight around the perimeter to correct off-center hits. If you're a highly skilled player, buy clubs with no perimeter weighting. If you are a less skilled player, opt for clubs with perimeter weighting.

Size

Size is another factor when buying irons. Put simply, the larger the club head, the easier it is to get entangled in the rough or a plush lie. The smaller the sole, the easier it is to get out of the rough or a plush lie. That's why many teaching pros recommend a mid- to wide-soled iron for clubs from 2 to 9, and more blade style irons for wedges. Blade style clubs improve your chances of hitting out of the rough or a plush lie while providing the ability to stop the ball quickly on the green. Consider buying blade style wedges if you often find yourself playing from the rough.

Heel-to-Toe Length

Heel-to-toe length is more cosmetic then anything else, although it somewhat affects forgiveness. Some players simply like the look of a more compact iron even though the longer heel-to-toe design offers a larger, more effective hitting area. If you want the maximum amount of forgiveness in your clubs, select ones with a longer heel-to-toe design.

Face Height

Face height is similar to heel-to-toe length. If you are looking for the most forgiving irons you can find, choose ones that have more face height.

Shafts

Poor ball flight pattern plagues many golfers. Poor pattern causes players to lose 3-5 strokes or more a round. The ideal is a high, penetrating shot that lands softly on the green or the fairway. Too low a ball flight pattern prevents you from stopping your shot where you want. Instead, the ball rolls off the green into trouble. Too high a ball flight pattern robs you of distance, preventing you from clearing hazards or from reaching the green on an approach shot. Poor ball flight pattern could be a sign that you don't have the right shaft for your clubs.

The shaft is a vital consideration when buying clubs. The key features of a shaft are flex, torque, length, and weight. If one of these features is off, it affects your swing, preventing your ball from achieving that high, penetrating shot we all want. Below is information on each of the key features of a shaft.

Flex

Flex is one of the most important, if not the most important, feature when selecting a shaft. Flex is the amount a club bends during the swing. The shaft's flex must match the player's swing speed for best results. If there's too much flex, the player has less control of the ball when hit. This player will have a tendency to draw or hook the ball. It there's not enough flex, the player loses distance but gains control. This player will have a tendency to fade or slice the ball.

Torque

Another important consideration is torque. Torque is the amount the club head twists when the player swings the club. Torque, like flex, must match the player's swing speed. To get the maximum distance and control from a shaft, you need to have the right torque rating. If you have a shaft with a rating of 2.5 stiff and you're hitting the ball 275 yards without roll, you're probably not getting the most out of your shaft. That's because you're not putting enough load on the shaft to maximize the club's torque rating. Without sufficient load, the shaft won't unload at its maximum capability.

Many players need help getting the clubhead to release properly through impact. That's where torque comes in. More torque, however, means less control of the club head when hitting the ball.

Shaft Weight

Weight affects how the club feels. Every golfer likes a different feel to his clubs. Some like clubs with their weight in the club head, others like clubs with their weight more evenly distributed. Some like irons with the weight in the club head, and woods with the weight evenly distributed. Others like irons with the weight evenly distributed and woods with the weight in the club head. It all depends on the feel. The feel of a club is important because it affects the player psychologically. That, in turn, affects his self-confidence.

Shaft Length

Do you often find yourself choking up on your clubs? Does your back hurt the morning after a round of golf? That's your body telling you your clubs are too long or too short. Your body changes its motion to compensate for the wrong size clubs. Using a new motion brings new muscles into play, stressing them and generating pain. This change also hampers your swing rhythm, a key to playing successful golf. Without good rhythm, the player will never develop a powerful swing.

If your clubs are too long, you'll see these types of shots:

- Low Hook
- Higher ball flight
- Fat shots
- Worm burners
- Push or Slice

Low Hook - The extra long shaft makes the club's toe stick up, causing the heel to grab the ball first. This development in turn creates right to left spin on the ball and lower ball flight.

Higher Ball Flight - Golfers often compensate for the additional length by standing too tall and leaning back on their downswing. Leaning back creates extra loft, causing a high shot with little distance.

Fat Shots - Because you have longer shafts you tend to compensate for the additional shaft length. But you forget to compensate about 40 percent of the time. This causes you to make contact with the ground a hair to soon, resulting in fat shots.

Worm Burner - This is the opposite of the fat shot. Here, you over compensate for shaft length by standing too tall. Instead of making solid contact with the ball, you hit the upper part of the ball, causing a worm burner or the low skimming shot that flies 60 yards over the green.

If your clubs are too short, you'll see these types of shots:

- Push or slice
- Catch the ball thin

Push or Slice - An iron that's too short points the toe into the ground, causing it to grab the ball too early in the swing. It also pushes your heel forward, which in turn generates left to right spin on the ball resulting in a push or a slice.

Catching It Thin - If you're hitting weak shots with little distance or height, you may be simply catching the ball too thin. That's a clear indication that the clubs are too short for you.

Graphite or Steel shafts?

It used to be that recreational golfers and those with a mid- and high-handicap would stick with the graphite while the more advanced players and low-handicappers would switch to steel. But times change and so did that mindset. Most pros have made the move from steel to graphite in recent years and in 2004 Tiger Woods joined them, switching to a graphite shaft in his driver.

When deciding whether or not you wish to make the switch from steel to graphite - or vice versa - there are some key differences between the two that you should note:

Key points

- Steel shafts are less expensive than graphite, meaning the cost of a steel set of clubs is substantially less than a graphite set of clubs.
- Graphite shafts are now as durable as steel shafts, though both have their weak points. Quality graphite shafts last a long time so long as they are not chipped or cracked, or the laminate-seal is not peeling. Steel shafts will last forever so long as they are not bent, rusted or pitted.
- You get less vibration in your hands with graphite shafts, and more vibrations with steel shafts. It depends on how much vibrations you

want. Some amateurs like the extra feedback that steel provides while many prefer as little vibration as possible. If you are prone to a lot of bad hits, your hands might be buzzing after a round with a steel shaft.

- Most important is the weight difference. Graphite shafts, and therefore graphite clubs, are much lighter than steel shafts and steel clubs.

In the ever-lasting quest to gain even precious yardage on their swing, many golfers have made the switch from steel to graphite. According to club-making and equipment guru Tom Wishon, you can gain an extra 6-12 yards of distance on your drive with graphite.

Before you say "Well that's it then, I'm switching to graphite" there are some other points you will want to consider:

Steel shafts are still very much a part of the great game of golf. Many players, namely low-handicappers and scratch players even prefer them. So do those big swingers who feel they don't need extra distance in their swing that a graphite shaft can provide. Many feel that a steel shaft gives them better control over their club head. Others like the added feedback (as we discussed) that comes from more vibrations up and down the shaft on a bad shot.

Tom Wishon himself says this: "If gaining more distance is a primary goal for the golfer, they should definitely be fit with the proper graphite shaft design in their woods and irons to match their swing. On the other hand, if distance is not the main focus for the golfer because they already have a high swing speed, if they like the feel of steel and their swing tempo matches a little better to the higher total weight steel shafts bring to the clubs, then steel is the better option."

It may be said that steel shafts are for steely players, those who are physically strong and have no problems in their hands, forearms or shoulders. Everyone else may want to go with graphite. There is no shame in making the choice because that's the way the majority go these days.

Grips

Once you reach a higher level, you need to understand the impact a golf grip has on your game.

Grip Size: A correct grip size is of utmost importance because it allows you to set the club properly at the top of your backswing. If the grip is too small, there will be too much hand action. This may lead to the clubface closing prematurely. If the grip is too big, it may restrict hand movement. You won't be able to close the club on time. Have a golf-professional or club-fitter check your size.

Grip Style: Your grip style is strictly a personal preference. Don't choose a style just because it's used by a well-known tour player. Choose a style that gives you confidence and good feel.

Replacing Grips: The time to replace a grip is when you no longer feel comfortable with the present one. Some grips wear off faster simply because you use those clubs more often. You should keep spares of the same kind of grips in your house.

Uniformity: If your driver is a different brand than your woods and irons, you will probably have different grips. As such, the feel is different each time you use a different grip. Try to have a uniform set of grips for all your clubs, except the putter.

Buying used Golf Clubs

Used clubs are a good alternative if you're on a budget. Sometimes you can find a great deal in used clubs. Many golfers like to test the latest equipment on the market. These are usually high-handicapped golfers with plenty of money to burn. What they want is to show off their gleaming new golf sets. To them 'Golf is for show'. These golfers would never be caught using sets more than a year old and they will gladly sell them to you cheaply. If you happen to know any such golfers, consider yourself lucky.

You may also find used sets which are quite suitable to your play. It's preferable to purchase a used set that suits you than to invest in a new set that isn't suitable.

You can often get a well-priced set advertised at your local driving range or in your newspapers classifieds. Don't buy the clubs blindly; take a close look at them first. In particular check the following:

Clubheads

Check for clubface wear. See whether there is a marked difference in the metal. If the center of the clubface is shinier, it's a good indication the club has been well used. Also check for grooves. Do they have well defined edges? If the center grooves are shallower than the rest, the clubhead has been worn down.

Examine the face at eye level. Do you notice a smooth surface or one with indentations? Avoid clubs with an irregular surface. You won't hit consistently.

Shafts

Any indentation on a shaft indicates a serious weakness. That part of the shaft has hit a hard object such as a tree, signpost, marker stakes or another club.

Scratches are often found near the hosel. They are usually caused by the clubhead of an adjacent club in the bag. This is an indication that the previous owner didn't take care of his clubs.

For graphite shafts, test the torque by twisting it in opposite directions. If it twists, it's useful life is over.

Some steel shafts have been bent back into shape. Look down the shaft to see this imperfection. Sometimes you can feel it.

Check for rust. Small specks or faint dots all over indicate the shaft has been polished to remove the rust spots.

Are all the shafts of the same make? A different shaft gives a different feel.

Grips

Expect some reasonable wear and tear. Check for cracks and tears. If you need to re-grip the whole set of clubs, a set isn't worth buying.

Set Consistency

Line up the clubs in order; there should be a half inch difference between each pair. Do they appear to come from the original set? Non-homogeneous clubs may not have a uniform progression of lofts throughout the set.

Check Current Prices

Find out the price of the equivalent new set of the model you're buying. Don't be surprised if there is little price difference, especially if the model has been discontinued by the manufacturer. You can use this info when haggling with the seller.

Try Them Out

Ask the seller to meet you at the local driving range, there you can try to hit a few balls and see if you are comfortable.

GOLF & BUSINESS

Since golf outings are now part of corporate life, your boss may ask you to entertain some foreign executives who want to spend Saturday morning playing golf instead of sightseeing. He may book a flight to an exclusive private club you only play in your dreams. You rub your hands with glee.

Playing golf with your regular buddies is one thing. Playing golf with a potential client is quite another. There is much more pressure and you are in uncharted waters. One wrong step could mean making coffee for the rest of your career.

Therefore, you should know some of the corporate rules of the game.

No Lying

Lying is the cardinal sin in corporate golf. Many golfers lie about their handicaps. If you claim to have a handicap of 26 instead of your real 22, you better play to the higher handicap. You may think this is easy. It's not. Not if you have sharp eyes watching your every swing.

Basic Etiquette

Of course, basic etiquette of the game applies. If you normally move about or talk when someone is teeing off, you better stop. The same goes for casting your shadow on to someone's putting line. Even failing to rake bunkers or repairing pitch marks may place you in a bad light.

Suddenly, that Saturday morning seems torturous and those perfect manicured fairways turn into microscope slides with you as a specimen. The Nassau represents your career future and you don't even know whether to win or to lose.

You should adopt the scout motto "Be Prepared".

You'll be dealing with many different characters – an executive who cheats, an aggressive vendor trying his sales pitch or an absent-minded elderly man who always forgets his club. At the end of the round, you'll find out more about them than in a full day business meeting.

As they say, "Golf tells no lies".

Remember that others will be finding out more about you. There are three microscopes focusing on you. Any silly behavior or remark could have an adverse effect on you and your career.

Business Talk?

Should you talk business on the golf course? This is the million dollar question.

Why not? That's why you're there in the first place.

The question should be *when*.

The answer, according to experts, is to leave this to the others in the group. Eventually one of them will start asking questions. They aren't here just to play golf. They'll make use of the casual atmosphere of the golf course to look at your bottom card.

When they ask questions, respond with short answers. Don't take this as an opportunity to make your sales pitch. Answer all the questions and then return to the casual atmosphere of the game.

Tact

It's good to know what your fellow golfers expect. When conversing with other players during a golf game, use the dialogue to find out about their handicaps. Are they serious golfers or are they here to enjoy the sun?

Whatever happens, you must be accommodating. At the same time, let them know they are here to enjoy a game of golf. If someone insists on talking about a product, politely remind him there's plenty of time to talk about that at the clubhouse. Remember most people are here to enjoy golf as well.

No Cheating

If it's not your day and you're playing badly, you may decide to cheat a little about your score. Good golfers have a keen eye and know how many strokes you have used for a hole. Entering a lower score is tantamount to covering up your work for minor errors.

If you happen to catch one of your foursome cheating on his score, what should you do? Cheating indicates that he isn't really honest. You now know what kind of a person you're dealing with. The best reaction is to appear unaware of his cheating. Never tell on him during the round. After all, the score isn't that important. You can advise your boss later.

Cell Phones

Many golf courses forbid the use of cell phones. They are one of the most annoying disturbances on the course. Unfortunately, many golfers still use them. If you have to have your cell phone with you, turn it off. Think of the outing as a board meeting. You don't want to answer or make a call in the middle of an important discussion.

Another equally distracting device is the Blackberry. If you find one of your foursome constantly thumbing through emails while others are waiting, you can be sure he's not interested in the game or you. Under such circumstances, it isn't impolite to remind him you are all here to play golf.

The key to a successful outing is to enjoy the occasion and strengthen relationships. However, don't think that just because you were invited to play golf with a group of top executives, you have landed a business deal. This may not be the case. Your fellow players may just be really keen golfers who genuinely want to enjoy a good game of golf. Your boss may not know that when he invites you to join them. He'll consider it a good company investment regardless.

Playing With Your Bosses

If you are asked to join the CEO or any superior for a round, you're looking at an informal interview for a promotion!

Senior executives are an exclusive group who rarely mix with employees lower down the ladder outside the office. These people are most likely wanting to know your character when they play with you. In the formal atmosphere of the office, your character is often veiled. Out in the open, they want to know you better.

Since most golfers experience first tee jitters, your first shot at the ball on the first tee is a test of your nerves. This translates to your first meeting with a potential client.

- Do you approach the ball calmly or you are still fighting to stop your body from shaking?

Surprisingly, where that ball goes isn't as important as how you hit it.

Not surprisingly, the crucial moment is on the green. This is when all of you are together. That simple putt becomes a test of your tenacity.

- Do you carefully aim and align again when your ball rolls two feet over the hole or do you tap it in nonchalantly?

- Do you congratulate a good ten-foot putt into the hole or do you scowl at it because you lost the hole?

They want to know your level of sportsmanship. This is important in business.

Avoid throwing your match away. Your boss will be watching for this. If you're caught doing it, you can be sure there will be no more golf outings.

They expect you to play to your handicap or somewhere around there. They will appreciate your effort to play well.

The last thing they want to see is a haphazard swing when they know you can do better.

VARIATIONS OF GOLF

Stroke Play

More than 90% of the golf tournaments you see on TV are played using the stroke play format.

Stroke play is a simple system. You record how many strokes you play on each hole. After the 18 holes, you total up the scores. All the scores of each competitor are compared and the lowest score is the winner.

On TV, you don't see the total of the ongoing scores on the board. Instead, you see the number of strokes in relation to the par. This score is written as 'Even' or 'Par', or it's a number with a plus or minus sign in front. Plus indicates the score is over par and minus indicates under.

If there is a tie at the end of the competition, a playoff is conducted for all the players concerned. A playoff can occur over one hole or another full round of 18 holes. If a winner is not decided after the playoff, a sudden death is played until one player emerges as the winner.

The four major tournaments employ different playoffs. The Masters employs a sudden death playoff. The PGA Championship uses a 3-hole playoff. The British Open uses a 4-hole playoff. The US Open requires participants to play another full round of 18 holes!

Match Play

There are only two basic forms of playing golf: stroke play and match play.

Both are decided by the number of strokes a golfer plays. In stroke play, the strokes are carried forward until the final hole. In match play, the strokes count ends after each hole.

In stroke play, you can play alone. You are competing against the course. In match play, you need someone to compete against. The Ryder Cup is probably the most famous golf competition in the world. The event uses match play.

Scoring in match play is simple.

You count the number of strokes you take to sink your ball into a hole. The same goes for your opponent.

- If you take fewer strokes than him, you win.
- If he takes fewer strokes than you, you lose.
- If both of you scores the same, the game is considered a tie.

Then you move on to the next hole. It's very simple and easy to remember.

You don't have to remember the number of strokes each of you has played in the preceding holes. In fact, you don't even have to remember the number of holes you have won or lost! You only need to remember the difference.

Scoring terminology goes like this:

- If you win the first hole, you're **One-up** and you proceed to the next hole.
- If your opponent wins, you're **All-square**.
- If you win, you're **Two-up** and your opponent is **Two-down**.

This continues until the last hole. If a holes ends in a tie, forget it. The score will always reflect the difference of the number of holes won and lost. If you're One-up after the last hole, you win the match.

Most times, the match will end before the last hole.

If you have won the first ten holes, there's no point continuing to play because your opponent can't win even if he wins the remaining holes.

This leads us to some interesting terminology that isn't found in stroke play.

Stableford

It started in Cheshire, England. While playing at the Wallasey Golf Club, an avid golfer reached a windy hole. He saw that one hole can jeopardize a golfer's decent score. This reminds him of something he had done years ago in Wales.

Dr. Frank Barney Gordon Stableford devised a system to eliminate the effects of a big score on the entire scorecard. After some modifications on the handicap, his system was tried out in 1932. The members of the Wallasey Golf Club embraced this system. Today, it's played by millions of golfers all over the world.

In Stableford, scoring points are awarded for a golfer's performance at each hole. These points are accumulated over 18 holes. Unlike stroke play, the golfer with the highest total number of points wins. Stableford formats are more popular in the UK than in the US. A modified form is used for professional tours.

The Stableford scoring as prescribed in Rule 32 of the Rules of Golf:

- **More than one over fixed score or no score**   0
- **One over fixed score**   1
- **Fixed Score**   2
- **One under fixed score**   3
- **Two under fixed score**   4
- **Three under fixed score**   5
- **Four under fixed score**   6

The "fixed score" is determined by the tournament committee. If the fixed score is set as par, then par scores 2 points and a double bogey scores 0.

In Stableford, some penalties imposed on a breach of rules differ from those in stroke play. In stroke play, a competitor is disqualified for having more than 14 clubs in his bag. In a Stableford competition, points are deducted instead. Pro Tournaments on the PGA and European Tour use a different scale of points when playing the Stableford format.

This is called the Modified Stableford and the points are as follows:

- **Double Bogey or worse**   -3
- **Bogey**   -1
- **Par**   0
- **Birdie**   2
- **Eagle**   5
- **Double Eagle (Albatross)**   8

As you can see, the Modified Stableford penalizes bad play, but offers higher rewards for great play. For the average golfer who usually has more bogeys than pars, the traditional Stableford is a preferable system.

Playing in Stableford competitions encourages golfers to take risks. This makes the competition more exciting. Since the worst you can get is a zero, why not go for it. The rewards for success outweigh the penalties for failure.

Take these hypothetical scores for two holes:

	Hole 1 (Par 4)		Hole 2 (Par 5)		Total	
	Stroke	**Stableford**	**Stroke**	**Stableford**	**Stroke**	**Stableford**
Player 1	4 (Par)	2	5 (Par)	2	9	4
Player 2	5 (+1)	1	4 (-1)	3	9	4
Player 3	6 (+2)	0	3 (-2)	4	9	4
Player 4	7 (+3)	0	2 (-3)	5	9	5

The above table shows there is no difference for the first three players whether they are playing stroke or Stableford. However, the 4th player returns a better score in Stableford.

The table below shows this performance using the Modified Stableford format:

	Hole 1 (Par 4)		Hole 2 (Par 5)		Total	
	Stroke	**M.S.**	**Stroke**	**M.S.**	**Stroke**	**M.S.**
Player 1	4 (Par)	0	5 (Par)	0	9	0
Player 2	5 (+1)	-1	4 (-1)	2	9	1
Player 3	6 (+2)	-3	3 (-2)	5	9	2
Player 4	7 (+3)	-3	2 (-3)	8	9	5

A steady prudent golfer (Player 1) is at a distinct disadvantage playing under this system.

As you can see, the difference is even higher. An eagle is worth a huge 5 points and a Double Eagle (Albatross) a massive 8 points. A birdie warrants 2 points as opposed to the bogey which penalizes only -1 point.

Consequently, you can expect to see a lot of exciting play and risk-taking in the Modified Stableford.

For amateur golfers, their net scores are used instead of their gross. This is in accordance with the USGA Handicap Manual.

POPULAR GOLF BETTING GAMES

There are many variations in golf to add more fun to the game. A little wager adds excitement and tension. While you're deciding how to hustle your fellow golfer, please take note that the PGA and the USGA don't condone gambling. Of course, deciding on who buys the next round of beer is perfectly acceptable.

1-2-3 Best Ball: This is a team competition format where each team is made up of 4 players. On the first hole, the lowest score of the four is taken. On the second hole, the sum of the two lowest scores is taken. On the third hole, the sum of the 3-lowest score is used. On the 4th hole, the cycle starts again. The team with the lowest total score wins. This format keeps all the players of the team involved.

Aces & Deuces: Sometimes called **Acey Ducey**, this is a betting game for 4 players. The reward for an ace (lowest score) and the penalty for a duece (highest score) is determined before the game. At each hole, the ace wins the reward from the other three. A deuce pays the penalty to the other three. If a tie occurs on the low score, nobody is an ace. Similarly, if a tie occurs on the high score nobody is a deuce.

Arnies: Named after Arnold Palmer, this is a side bet during a game. The player who manages to make par or better without hitting his ball into the fairway wins the bet.

Add-On: An agreement between two teams. When one team loses by a predetermined number of games in a match, a new match begins concurrently. This gives the losing team a chance to recoup some of his loses or lose more.

Bag Raid or Pick Up Sticks: A match play format game between two players. It's fun and simple to play. Each time you win a hole, your opponent takes one club away from your bag.   He can choose any club except the putter. For the rest of the round, you play without that club. Normally a 9-hole round decides the winner. Bag Raid is a good game for training creative shots.

Best Ball: A match play format game for 2-4 players. The best ball is the player with the lowest score.

Bingle-Bangle-Bungle: A fun competition where each hole offers 3 points. The first point is awarded to the player who first hits the green. When all the balls are on the green, the second points goes to the ball nearest the hole. The last point goes to the first ball to go into the hole. This is a great game for golfers of different skill levels.

Birdies: This is a game where players receive points for birdies. In some variations, one point is given for a net birdie and two for a gross birdie.

Blind Bogey: This is a format used for tournaments. There are many variations of Blind Bogey including the following:

- All golfers play 18 holes of stroke play. After the round ends, the tournament director randomly picks a number from a bag. Any golfer(s) whose score matches the number wins. If no one matches the number, another number is picked or the golfer(s) closest to the number wins.

- Before the rounds begins, golfers choose a number as their handicap. This number is recorded by the tournament director to guard against cheating later. After the round, the tournament randomly picks a number. The golfers whose net score matches that number win.

- Everyone tees off. At the end of the round, the tournament selects six random holes. The scores of these six holes are discarded. The remaining 12 holes are totaled. The lowest score wins.

Bloodbath: A foursomes play format. Everyone tees off. You choose which of your opponent's balls they will continue to play. The same goes for your opponents – they'll decide which ball you'll play.

Chapman: see **Pinehurst**.

Chicago: A valid handicap is needed for this game. One point is awarded for a bogey, two for a par, four for a birdie, eight for an eagle and sixteen for a double eagle or albatross. The points are all added up, including the handicap. The player with the highest points wins.

Flags: This is a side bet for par-3 holes. A reward is given for a player whose ball lies within a certain distance (usually the length of a standard putter) from the flag.

Fourball: A form of team golf where two pairs compete against each other. Each player plays his own ball. Each team chooses its best score at the end of the hole. The lower score wins.

Foursomes: A team match play format where each team plays with one ball.

Team members decide beforehand who will tee off from the odd-numbered hole and who will use the even-numbered holes. After the tee-off, play continues with players hitting alternately until the ball is holed.

This game is also called **Alternate Shot**.

Freebies: Also called **mulligan**, a player is allowed a chance to replay a shot if he elects to do so. However, once he decides to play a freebie, the previous shot is cancelled. His freebie shot will count even if it's worse than his previous shot.

Freebies are quite popular in social or charity tournaments where a player can buy any number of freebies per round. The proceeds collected from the sales of such freebies are donated to charity.

Got'cha: A game where a player can demand that his opponent replay his shot. The maximum number of such replays is usually four.

Greenies: A side bet where a player or team is rewarded for hitting closest to the green on a par-3 hole.

Hawk: This is another fun game. Before teeing off, players draw numbers from 1-4 to determine playing order. This order cycle remains unchanged throughout the game. For the first hole, the player drawing #1 is the hawk and has the honor of teeing off first.

Once everyone has teed off, the hawk can choose a partner for the current hole or he can choose to play alone. In this case, if the hawk wins, he receives 3 points. Otherwise, each of his opponents receives 1 point. If the hawk chooses a partner, the best ball decides. The team that wins collects a point each.

The honor for the next hole goes to the player with the lowest score. The hitting order remains. If player #3 scores the lowest, he becomes the hawk for the next hole. The tee-off order will be 3-4-1-2. The game continues in the same format.

Highs & Lows: In this team game, two points are awarded for each hole. The first point goes to the team with the lower total score. The second point goes to the team whose individual high score is lower than the opponent's individual high score. If there is a tie, the points are carried forward to the next hole.

Low Ball / Low Total: A team game in which one point is awarded to the lowest individual score and one point to the lowest combined score of each team. If there is a tie, the points are carried over to the next hole.

Mulligan: see **Freebies**.

Nassau: This is a very popular betting game. Three pots are to be won. The first pot goes to the player who scores the lowest for the front nine. The second pot goes to the player who scores the lowest for the back nine. The third pot goes to the player who scores the lowest for the 18 holes. A slight variation is two pots for the lowest score for 18 holes.

Nines: This is a game for a threesome. Nine points are awarded on each hole: 5 for the lowest score, 3 for the middle score and 1 for the highest score. If there is a tie, the points are added up and divided equally amongst the players. At the end of the round, the player with the highest total points wins.

Pick Up Sticks: see **Bag Raid**.

Pinehurst: Also called the **Chapman,** this is a team match play game. In this format, both players of each team tee off with their own balls. On the second shot, each uses their partner's ball. For the third shot, they select the ball in a better position and play an alternate shot format for that hole.

Sandies: A side bet where a point is awarded to a player who gets up and down from a greenside bunker.

Scramble: This is a popular format in pro-am competitions. Each team consists of 4 members. Each player drives and the team captain decides which ball is in the best position. Then each member of that team plays from that spot or within a foot of it. The process continues until the ball goes into the hole.

In a variation of the above, each member must drive at least a preset number of times, usually four. This adds more excitement and involves strategy.

Sixes: Sometimes called **Hollywood** or **Round Robin**, this is a game for four players. It pits members against one another 2 on 2. However, players change partners after every six holes. This way, every player partners every other player over 18 holes. 1 point is awarded for each six-hole set.

Six, Six & Six: A team game in which the format changes after every 6 holes. The first 6 holes are played using the fourball format. The second 6 holes use the foursomes or alternate shot. For the last 6 holes, each plays his own ball with the lower combined score as the winner for each hole.

Skins: This game gained popularity because of the Skins games on TV. A skin (reward) is awarded to the player with the lowest score for each hole. If there is a tie, the skin is carried over to the next game. This continues until there is an outright winner. A variation is a progressive increase of the skin through the holes.

Snake: This is a side bet in which the first player to 3-putt or more gets the "snake". He must keep it until someone else three-putts when the snake changes hands. The player holding the snake at the end of the round buys the beer.

Stableford: This is a very common format in tournament play. Points are awarded for each hole's performance. A typical breakdown is: bogey (1), par (2), birdie (3), eagle (4) and double eagle or albatross (5). The player with the highest total points wins.

A modified stableford format is used for the International on the PGA Tour.

String: A betting game where each player is issued a string of a given length, such as 10 feet, before the game. During the game, a player can use all or part of his string to move his ball anywhere within the length of the string anytime. For example, if your ball is 10 feet from the hole, you can use the entire length of the string and you don't have to putt. However, each time you use any part of the string, you have to cut off the length you use. You need to use your string wisely.

Three-Ball: This is a game for 3 players in which each player competes against the other two individually.

Threesomes: A match in which one player plays against the team of two players who play alternate shots.

Watson: A side bet in which a player gets a reward for holing a shot from outside the green.

Wolf: This game is for four. Players rotate in becoming the "wolf" who tees off first. Before doing so, he has to announce one of two options: 1 against 3 or 2 on 2. If he chooses 2 on 2, he must choose his partner immediately after that player's drive. If he has not made his choice before the last player tees off, he has to partner the last player.

For a 2 on 2, the side with the lowest better ball score wins the hole and receives 1 point each. For a 1 against 3, the wolf's score is used against the lowest score of the other three. If he wins, he gets 3 points. If he loses, the other 3 players gets a point each. Ties carry no points.

Wolfman: This is a betting game for 3 players. The player whose tee-off distance is between the other two is the "wolfman" and the other two are the "hunters". The hole is played out individually. The hunters' scores are added while the wolfman's score is doubled. If the wolfman's score is lower, he wins. If it's higher, he loses.

Worst-Ball: In this long drawn game format between two teams, every player tees off. The team plays the next shot from the ball that's in the worst position or "scramble" style. This continues until a team holes out. The team with the lowest score wins a point.

GOLF GLOSSARY

There are so many terms in golf that it's impossible to include all of them in this book. Below are just some of the terms you will encounter as you become more involved with this game:

Ace: A hole-in-one. To sink the ball into the hole right from the tee-off.

Acceleration: An increase in speed most often associated with the hands, arms or club.

Address: The position taken by a golfer as he is about to hit the ball.

Advice: Instructions on how to play a ball.

Aggregate: The total score of members of a team. In a multi-round competition, the total score of each round.

Aiming: The act of aligning the clubface to the target.

Air Shot: A golf shot that misses the ball completely

Albatross: A score of three strokes under par. Also called a 'Double Eagle'.

Alternate Ball: A competition format in which players take alternate turns to hit the ball. Also called Foursomes.

Amateur: A golfer who plays without cash rewards.

Angle Of Approach: The angle at which the club moves downward towards the ball.

Approach Shot: A shot designed to send the ball to the putting green.

Apron: The piece of ground surrounding the putting green. Also called the fringe (see picture)

Attack: An aggressive play.

Attend The Flag: Action of holding the flag and then removing it while another golfer plays.

Away: The ball that is farthest from the hole when there are two or more.

Back Door: The back end of the hole.

Back Lip: The sloping part of a bunker farthest to the green.

Back Nine: Holes #10 through #18.

Baffle: A 5-wood.

Ball at Rest: A ball that is not moving.

Ball Embedded: A golf ball that is stuck into the ground

Ball Holed: A ball that has gone completely below the level of the lip of the hole.

Ball In Play: A ball is in play once the player has made a stroke on it at the tee box. It remains in play until it is holed out, lost, out of bounds, lifted or substituted.

Ball Marker: Anything that is used to indicate the position of a golf ball.

Ball Retriever: A long pole with a scoop at the end that is used to fetch a ball

Ball Washer: A machine for cleaning golf balls (see picture on the right).

Banana Ball: A ball that curves a lot to the right in the shape of a banana.

Baseball Grip: A grip that utilizes all ten fingers.

Bend One: To curve a ball.

Bent grass: A hardy and resilient grass of the *genus Agrostis* that is native to North America and Eurasia.

Bermuda: A type of grass of the genus *Cynodon dactylon* that is native to southern Europe.

Best Ball:

- A match in which one player plays against the better score of two balls or the best score of three players.
- The better score of two partners in a four-ball or best-ball match.

Better Ball: A match play or stroke play game where two players on one side play their own ball throughout the round. The low score or better ball among the two on each hole is the team's score for a hole.

Birdie: A score of one score under par for a hole.

Blade: The clubhead of a golf iron apart from the hosel.

Blade Putter: A putter with its basic head form similar to the other standard irons (see picture on right).

Blind Bogey: A competition format in which each player tries to score closest to a random score.

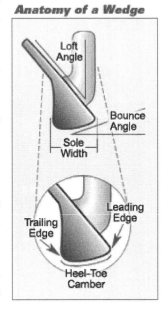

Blind Hole: A hole on the putting green that is not visible to the player.

Block: A poor shot that is struck late in the swing.

Bogey: A score of one over par for the hole.

Bogey Competition: A competition format where players play against a fixed score at each hole.

Bounce: The angle of the leading edge of a club's sole and the ground. Bounce is most commonly applied to wedges.

Boundary: The edge of a golf course.

Bowker: A lucky shot that is going astray but hits something such as a tree, rock or spectator, and bounces back into play.

Bramble: A molded surface used on early golf balls.

Brassie: A former name given to a 2-wood. The hitting surface is made of brass.

Break

- To score less than a specified number. Eg. "Try to break 90."
- The turning point of a ball rolling on a slope on a green.
- The bending of the wrists during a swing.

Bulge: The curved surface of a wood club.

Bulger: A wood club with a curved surface such as a driver.

Bump & Run: A shot in which the ball bounces and rolls some distance.

Bunker: A depression in the ground that is covered with sand. Also called a 'sand trap'.

Buried Ball: A ball that is either partially or fully covered by the sand in a bunker.

Caddie: A person who carries a player's clubs and offers advice.

Caddie Master: A person who is in charge of the caddies.

Can: To make a putt.

Card: **1**. To make a score. **2**. A golfer's score card.

Carpet: A slang term referring to the putting green or fairway in a golf course.

Carry: The distance traveled by a golf ball before it touches the ground.

Cart : A vehicle used to transport golfers and their equipment on the course.

Casting: A premature uncocking or unhinging of the wrists on the downswing. Also known as 'hitting from the top'.

Casual Water: A temporary accumulation of water usually caused by rain or a water sprinkler. This is not a hazard and a player is allowed to lift his ball and play from another spot without penalty.

Center Shafted: A putter in which the shaft is joined to the center of the head.

Charge: **1**. To come from behind. **2**. To play aggressively.

Chicken Wing: A swing flaw where the left elbow (for a right-hander) bends at an angle pointed away from the body.

Chili-Dip: To strike the ground before the ball during a chip shot.

Chip Shot: A short low approach shot.

Chip-And-Run: A chip shot that enables the ball to roll some distance on the green. Also known as "bump and run".

Chip In: To send the ball with a chip shot into the hole

Choke:

- To grip a club farther down the handle.
- Slang used to indicate a failed performance under pressure.

Chop: To hit the ball with a quick downward motion.

Chunk: To strike the ground well behind the ball.

Claggy: A lie that is a bit wet and muddy.

Claim: In match play, a protest by a player concerning a possible breach of the rules.

Cleat : The spike on the sole of a golf shoe (see picture on the right)

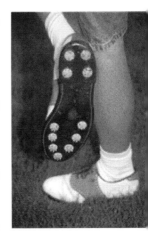

Cleek:

- A narrow-bladed iron used for long shots from the rough or sand
- A name for the 4-wood or 1-iron.

Closed Face: When the clubface is pointed toward the left of the target.

Closed Stance: A position of the player whose leading foot is nearer the target line during address.

Club:

- The implement used to strike the golf ball consisting of the grip, the shaft & the head.
- An organization or association of golfers.

Clubface: The hitting area of the club.

Club Professional : A professional who works for a golf club as a teacher and equipment supplier and plays only in local events.

Clubhouse: The main building on the golf course.

Clubhouse Lawyer: A derogatory term used for a person who appoints himself as an arbiter of the rules.

Cock: To bend the wrists backwards in the backswing.

Coefficient Of Restitution (COR): The ratio of the clubhead speed at impact to the velocity of the ball after it has been struck. The USGA imposed a limit of 0.83 on the COR in 1998.

Collar: The grassy fringe or apron surrounding the putting green.

Colorball: A team game with teams of 3-4 players where one player plays with a colored ball. The score for the team is the sum of the colored ball's score and the best score of the others. For the next hole, another player plays the colored ball. The order of play of the colored ball is decided before the competition.

Come Back Shot: A shot played after overshooting the hole.

Committee: The name given to the group of people in charge of a competition or a course.

Compression:

- The deformation of the ball against the clubface on impact.
- The degree of resilience of a golf ball.

Condor: A near impossible hole-in-one shot that can only happen in a par-5 hole. Also called a 'triple eagle'.

Control Shot : A shot that is played with less than full power.

Core: The center of the golf ball.

Course: The entire playing area for the game of golf.

Course Rating: A number expressed in strokes and decimal fractions of a stroke that indicates the number of strokes an average scratch player will take to complete a round from a given tee.

Crack: A condition in which a player's play deteriorates under pressure.

Cross-Bunker: A lengthy bunker that lies across the fairway.

Cup: The container in the hole that holds the flagstick in place.

Cut : A score that reduces the field to a pre-determined number; usually determined after half the number of required holes to be played in a tournament. To remain in a tournament, a player's score must be equal or lower than the cut.

Cut Shot : A controlled shot that makes a ball stop almost instantly on the green.

Dawn Patrol: Golfers who tee off early in the morning to avoid heavy traffic.

Dead: A description of a shot that stops immediately when it lands.

Dead Ball: A ball that is so close to the hole that there is no doubt it will be holed with the next putt.

Deep-Faced Club: A club with a clubface that is relatively thick from top to bottom.

Deuce: A hole made in two strokes.

Dew Sweepers: The first groups of golfers on the course in the morning.

Dimple: Indentation on the golf ball designed to improve its aerodynamics.

Divot : A piece of turf removed by the club when a shot is made.

Dogleg: A bend in the fairway.

Dormie: In match play, a situation in which a golfer is ahead by as many holes that remain. Sometimes spelled 'dormy'.

Double Bogey: A score of two over par for a hole.

Double Eagle: A score of three under par for a hole. Also called an 'albatross'.

Down: The number of holes or strokes a player is behind an opponent.

Downhill Lie: A position of the ball on a slope in which a right-handed golfer's left foot is lower than his right foot.

Downswing: The downward movement of a golfer's club toward the ball.

DQ'd: Short form of the word 'disqualified'.

Draw:

- The pairing of golfers for a match play.
- A controlled shot that curves from right to left for a right-handed player.

Drive: To hit a golf ball a long distance, usually with a driver.

Driver: The longest hitting club used primarily from the tee. Also known as the "1-wood".

Driving Iron: An iron club with a loft of approximately 17 degrees, a lie of approximately 56 degrees and a length of 39 inches. Also called a "One iron".

Driving Range: A place with facilities for golfers to practice.

Drop: To put a ball in play on the course after it has been declared unplayable or has been lost.

Dub: A missed or poorly hit shot.

Duff: To mishit the ball by striking the ground behind the ball first.

Duffer: An unskilled golfer. Also called a 'hacker'.

Dunk: To hit the ball into a water hazard.

Eagle: Two strokes under par for a hole.

Equator: The center line of a ball

Equipment: Anything used, carried or worn by a player. A ball in play is not considered equipment.

Etiquette: A set of guidelines to promote proper behavior on the course.

Executive Course: A golf course consisting mainly of par threes and very short par fours.

Explode: The action of the club spraying a large amount of sand in a bunker. Also called a "blast".

Explosion Shot: A shot out of a bunker that takes a great deal of sand with it.

Extra Hole: A hole played after a regulation round or match to break a tie.

Face: The hitting area or surface of the club.

Fade: A controlled shot in which the ball curves slightly from left to right when hit by a right-handed golfer.

Fairway: The area of the course between the tee box and the green that affords a good lie for the ball.

Fairway Wood: A wood club designed to hit the ball off the fairway.

Fan: To swing and completely miss the ball.

Fat Shot: A shot in which the club hits the ground before it hits the ball.

Feather: To hit a shot that lands lightly on the green with little roll.

Featherie: An early handcrafted golf ball made of stuffed feathers wrapped with leather.

Field: Players in a tournament.

Flag: Short for flagstick.

Flagstick: The removable marker placed in the hole to show its location.

Flange: The base of a club or the part that rests on the ground.

Flash Trap: A small, shallow sand trap.

Flat Swing: A swing in which the club is carried back at a relatively low angle to the ground.

Flex: The degree a club's shaft bends upon impact with the ball.

Flier: A shot hit with little or no spin that travels farther than normal.

Flier Lie: A ball sitting on top of the grass in a rough.

Flight:

- The trajectory of a ball in motion.
- A division of players of relatively equal standard in a tournament.

Flip Shot: A short shot of high trajectory played with a highly lofted club.

Flub: A poor shot caused by hitting the ground before the ball.

Follow-Through: The part of the swing after the ball has been struck.

Fore: The standard warning call in golf to those in danger of being hit by a ball.

Forecaddie: A person employed by the course or tournament committee to mark the position of a player's ball.

Four-Ball: A match in which the better ball of two players is played against the better ball of their opponents.

Foursomes: A match between two teams of two players each. Each team plays one ball with partners alternating shots.

Free Drop: A ball dropped without penalty into another area.

Fried Egg: A lie in which the ball is buried in sand.

Fringe: An area surrounding the putting green. Also called an 'apron'.

Frog Hair: Short grass bordering the edge of the green.

Front Nine: Holes #1 through #9. Also called "Front side".

Full House: A game in which a player is set a points target calculated by deducting his handicap from 36. The winner is the player who surpasses his target by the most points. Score is 8 points for an eagle, 4 for a birdie, 2 for a par and 1 for a bogey.

Gallery: Spectators of a golf tournament or the area for spectators.

Gimmie: A short putt that is likely to be conceded by the opponent.

Glove: A hand item worn by a golfer to improve the grip.

Goose Neck: A club in which the neck is slightly curved so that the heel is offset from the line of the shaft.

Graphite: A light carbon based material used to make shafts and clubheads.

Grain: The direction in which the grass on the green is growing.

Grand Slam: Winning all four major tournaments: British Open, US Open, PGA Championship and the Masters.

Grasscutter: A hard-hit low flying shot.

Green: Commonly used for the well-defined area where the hole is located.

Green Committee: Members of a golf club overseeing the management and maintenance of the course.

Green Fee: Payment to be made for the use of a golf course.

Green In Regulation: The number of shots taken when the ball stops on the green that is two less than the par of the hole.

Green Jacket: The mantle of honor given to the winner of the US Masters.

Greenkeeper: Employee of a club in charge of course maintenance.

Grip:

- The area of the shaft where the club is held.
- The manner in which a player grasps and holds the club.

Groove: Line scored on the face of a club.

Gross: The number of strokes played by a golfer before deducting his handicap.

Ground Under Repair (GUR): The area of the course that is being repaired. A ball lying in this area can be lifted without penalty (see picture)

Ground the Club: To touch the head of the ground on the ground during address.

Gutta Percha: The rubbery material used to make golf balls from 1948 until early 1900.

Guttie: A golf ball made of gutta percha.

Hack:

- To strike violently at the ball.
- To make bad shots.
- To play bad golf.

Hacker: An unskilled golfer. Also called a 'Duffer'.

Half / Halved: When the score is tied on a hole in match play.

Handicap: The number of strokes a player may deduct from his actual score. Designed to allow golfers of different abilities to compete on the same level.

Handicap Certificate: A document issued by a player's home club or golf association that indicates his current handicap

Handicap Golfer: An amateur golfer whose average score is above par and who is given a handicap in amateur competitions.

Hanging Lie: A ball resting on a downhill slope.

Hazard: A well-defined area in a golf course that is designed to make play more difficult.

Head: The part of the club that comes into contact with the ball.

Heel: The part of the clubhead that is closer to the player.

Hickory: Wood from a native North American tree. Used for making club shafts at the beginning of the 19th century.

Hit: To strike a golf ball.

Hitting From The Top: See 'Casting'.

Hog's Back: A ridge of ground or a hole having a ridge on a fairway.

Hold: To hit the ground and stay in place with little roll or bounce.

Hole:

- A 4¼" (108 mm) round receptacle in the green, at least 4" deep.
- A defined area starting from the tee box to the green.

Hole High: A ball that is even with the hole, but off to one side.

Hole In One: A hole made with one stroke. Same as an 'Ace'.

Hole Out: To complete play on a hole by hitting the ball into the cup.

Holed: The rules of golf state that a ball is only considered 'holed' when it lies within the circumference of the hole and is entirely below the level of the lip.

Home Green: The green on the last hole of the course.

Home Pro: A professional who holds a position at a golf club, teaches, and plays only in local events

Honor: The privilege of teeing off first on the tee box. This goes to the winner of the preceding hole. On the first tee, this is usually decided by drawing lots.

Hook: An uncontrollable ball that curves from right to left for a right-handed player.

Hosel: The part of the clubhead where the shaft is fitted.

Hustler: A skillful golfer who deliberately maintains a higher handicap than he's entitled to win bets.

hosel

In: The second 9 holes on a course – holes 10 to 18.

In Play: A ball that is not out of bounds.

Impact: The instantaneous moment when the clubhead meets the ball.

Inside: Being nearer the hole than the ball of your opponent.

Interlocking Grip: A grip in which the left little finger is intertwined with the right index finger for a right-handed golfer.

In The Leather: A putting distance not greater than the leather wrapping on the player's grip to the clubhead. In friendly play, players often concede such putts.

Intended Line: The line a player expects his ball to travel when hit.

Iron: One of the number of clubs with heads made of iron or steel.

Jerk: To hit the ball out of a bad lie with a downward cutting motion.

Jungle: Heavy rough.

Kick: An unpredictable or erratic bounce of the golf ball.

Lag: A long putt with the intention of getting the ball near the hole so that it can be holed with the next putt.

Lateral Hazard: A hazard that runs parallel to the line of play, usually alongside the fairway.

Lay Up: To hit a safe shot that stops short of a hazard.

Leading Foot: The foot nearer to the target. The left foot for a right-handed player (see picture on right).

Leading Hand: The hand nearer to the target. The left hand for a right-handed player.

Leader Board: A display of the leading golfers and their scores during a tournament.

Leading Foot

Lie: The position of a golf ball when it comes to rest.

Line: The path to be traveled by a golf ball.

Line Up: To determine the direction the ball should travel.

Links: Originally referred to a seaside course, but now refers to any golf course.

Lip: The upper rim of the hole.

Lob Shot: A shot that makes the ball go maximum height and minimum distance. Used when a player has to hit over an obstacle and has very little green to work with.

Local Rules: Rules established for a club by its own members.

Loft:

- The angle between the clubface and the vertical.
- The height of the ball when it is hit into the air.

Long Game: The part of the game where distance is important.

Long Irons: Irons with lesser loft that hit the ball lower and farther.

Loose Impediment: Natural objects that are not fixed, growing or sticking to the ball. Examples of loose impediments are leaves, twigs, insects and stones.

Lost Ball: A ball is considered lost if:

- It can't be found within five minutes after search begins.
- The player declares it lost before the five minutes of search.
- The player can't identify a ball which is found within five minutes as his.

LPGA: The Ladies' Professional Golf Association.

Make The Cut: To qualify for the final rounds of a tournament.

Mallet: A putter that has a head that is much wider and heavier than that of a blade putter.

Marker: A small object used to mark the spot before it is lifted.

Markers: Objects placed at the teeing ground to define the area in which players must tee their balls.

Marshal: A tournament official whose duty is to keep order among the spectators.

Match Play: A competition format that is determined by the number of holes won instead of the number of strokes.

Meadowland: A lush grassland course.

Medal Play: A competition decided by the overall number of strokes used to complete the round or rounds. Same as 'stroke play'.

Middle Wedge: An iron with a loft that is between that of a pitching wedge and a sand wedge.

Mid-Iron: A middle range iron, usually #5 through #7.

Mis-Club: To use the wrong club for the shot.

Mis-Hit: A term used when the clubhead did not hit the ball correctly.

Mis-Read: To read the line of putt wrongly. Mis-reading the green is a very common thing among all golfers.

Mixed Foursome: A foursome with each side consisting of a male and female player.

Model Swing: A completely professional swing.

Muff: To mis-hit a shot.

Mulligan: A special allowance where a player can replay a shot. Mulligans are not allowed in a proper tournament, but are popular in charity or social tournaments where players can purchase any number of them during a round.

Municipal Course: A public course owned by local government.

Nassau: A 3-part wager comprising of the front nine, the back nine and the complete round of 18 holes.

Neck – The part where the shaft of the club joins the head.

Net: A player's score after deducting his handicap.

Nine: A series of 9-holes.

Nineteenth Hole: The bar at the clubhouse.

Observer: An official who watches the competitors in a tournament and reports any breach of rules to the referee.

Obstruction: An artificial object that obstructs play.

Off-Centre: A ball that is not struck at the center of the clubface.

Offset: A club with its head set behind the shaft.

One Up: A match play term meaning a player has won one hole more than his opponent.

One-Iron: An iron club with a loft of approximately 17 degrees, a lie of approximately 56 degrees and a length of 39 inches. Also called a 'driving iron'.

One-Putt: To hole the ball with just one stroke of the putter when on the green.

One-Wood: Another name for a driver.

Open: A tournament where both amateurs and professions can participate.

Open Stance: A position during address where the front foot is farther from the target line than the back foot. This stance is often used to play a fade ball.

Out: The front nine holes – holes #1 through #9.

Out Of Bounds (OB): The region which lies outside a well-defined boundary. A player is prohibited to play in this region for that particular hole. A penalty is imposed on a player who hits a ball out of bounds. (See Rules).

Outside Agency: Anything that is not part of the match or anyone not part of the competitors' side in stroke play such as observers, forecaddies and referee.

Over Clubbing: To use a club which gives more distance than intended.

Over Par: A score higher than the indicated par for a hole or a round.

Overlapping Grip: A grip used by a player when the little finger of his trailing hand overlaps the space between the forefinger and the second finger of his leading hand. Also called the "Vardon Grip".

Pair:

- Two golfers playing together in a competition.
- To assign players to form a team partnership in match play.

Par: The number of strokes a scratch player should take to complete a hole. The course par is the total of all the hole pars.

Parkland: A course laid out in grassland with little rough.

Partner:

- One of two or more players on the same team in a match
- A player who plays together with another in a match.

Peg: A golf tee.

Penalty Stroke: An additional stroke added to a player's score for a breach of the rules.

PGA: Professional Golfers Association.

Pick Up: To take the ball before holing out. In match play, the player concedes the hole to his opponent. In stroke play, the player is disqualified.

Pin: A flagstick.

Pin-High: See 'Hole-High'.

Pin Placement: The location of the hole on a putting green.

Pin Position: Same as 'Pin Placement'.

Pitch: A shot that sends the ball high toward the green.

Pinsetter: The person who is responsible for pin placement.

Pitch And Run: A type of pitch shot that is lower and with less backspin that enables the ball to roll more after it lands on the green.

Pitching Niblick: An obsolete name for the 8-iron.

Pitching Wedge: An iron with a heavy flange designed to hit balls high.

Pivot: The act of rotating the hips, truck and shoulders during a swing.

Play-Off: The process of playing additional holes to determine the winner of a competition that ends in a tie.

Play Through: To overtake a group of golfer playing ahead. Golf etiquette dictates that a slower group should signal a faster group to play through.

Playing Professional: A professional golfer who primarily competes in tournaments

Plugged Lie: A lie in which the ball is buried in sand.

Plus Handicap: A player whose average is less than par. During a tournament, an amateur must add strokes to his gross to determine his net score.

Pop Up: A short, high shot.

Pot Bunker: A small deep sand trap that has steep sides.

Practice Green: A green set up for putting practice.

Preferred Lie: Under local rules, a manner in which a player is allowed to improve his lie without incurring a penalty.

Press: An extra bet on the remaining holes of a round.

Pro Shop: A shop at the golf club where golfing equipment is sold.

Pro-Am: A tournament where a professional is partnered with an amateur.

Professional: A player who plays for money. Abbreviated to 'Pro'.

Provisional Ball: A second ball played immediately after the first if the player thinks his first ball may be out of bounds or lost. If the first ball is found or found to be in play, it is played. Otherwise, the player continues to play with the provisional ball.

Pull: A shot that sends the ball relatively straight, but to the right of the target for a right-handed player.

Punch: A low, controlled shot hit into the wind.

Putt: A shot played toward the hole when the ball is on the putting green.

Putter: A club specially designed for putting.

Putting Green: The defined area that is specially prepared for putting.

Putting Surface: Same as 'Putting Green'.

Quail High: A shot that has a low and flat trajectory.

Quarter Shot: A shot that is made with less than a half swing.

Quitting On The Ball: Not hitting through the shot.

R & A: The Royal and Ancient Golf Club of St Andrews who oversees golf in Europe, Asia and the Commonwealth.

Rabbit: A touring professional who has to compete in qualifying rounds in order to play in tournaments.

Rake: A device used for smoothing the sand in a bunker.

Range: A practice area.

Recover: To play back into a satisfactory position on the fairway or green after hitting into an undesirable position.

Recovery Shot: A shot that is recovered. See above.

Release: The movement of a golfer's hands during a swing.

Relief: To drop the ball with penalty in accordance with the rules.

Reverse Overlap: For a right-handed player, a putting grip in which the index finger of his right hand overlaps the little finger of his left.

Rifle: To play a long distance shot with great accuracy.

Rim: The edge of the cup.

Rim Out: To run around the edge of the cup and fail to fall in.

Roll-On-A-Shot: Too much turning of the wrist at impact.

Rough: Long grass next to the fairway or hazards.

Round: A series of 18 holes.

Round Robin: A tournament in which each player plays against each other.

Rub Of The Green: A deflection or stopping of the ball in play caused by an outside agency, and for which no relief is given. In other words, bad luck.

Run: The distance the ball rolls on the ground.

Running Iron: A club used for making short running shots.

Run-Up: An approach shot that is close to or on the ground.

Sandbagger: A person who lies about their ability to gain an edge in the game – in other words, a cheat.

Sand Iron: An early heavy lofted club that was used for playing from bunkers. No longer in use.

Sand Trap: Another name for a bunker.

Sand Wedge: An iron with a heavy flange on the bottom that is specially designed to get the ball out of bunkers.

Sandy Par: Making par from a bunker.

Scoop: An improper swing with a digging or spooning action.

Scotch Foursome: A match where partners take alternating turns at shots. Each hole is started alternatively as well.

Scramble: A team competition in which every team members play from the position of the best ball of a team member after every stroke.

Scratch: A player without a handicap or whose handicap is zero.

Scratch Player: A golfer who does not require a handicap. All professional golfers are scratch players.

Second Ball: A situation can arise where a question over the legality of the ball in play cannot be settled by a referee or other members of the group. In this case, a second ball is played. The play completes that hole with two balls. The score of whichever ball is deemed legal at a post-match adjudication is used.

Scruff: To mishit the ball by grazing the ground with the clubhead before hitting the ball.

Semi-Private Course: A course that has members but is open to the public.

Set: A collection of golf clubs.

Set-Up: The series of preparations a player takes before his swing.

Shaft: The part of the golf club that is connected to the head.

Shag Bag: A bag for carrying practice balls.

Shagging: To collect balls from a practice area.

Shank: A shot struck by the club's hosel.

Shiperio: Similar to a mulligan, but the player is allowed to choose which ball to continue for the rest of the hole.

Short Game: The part of the game consisting of pitching, chipping and putting.

Short Irons: The higher lofted irons; usually from #8 through the wedges.

Shotgun: A tournament where all players start at different holes and at the same time. The origin of such a tournament may have been started by the firing of a shotgun.

Shot Hole: A par three hole.

Shotmaker: A player who has the ability to play a variety of shots.

Shotmaking; Playing a variant shot that warrants the given situation.

Side: A team.

Side hill Lie: A lie with the ball either above or below your feet.

Single: A match involving two players, one against the other.

Sink A Putt: To the ball into the hole.

Skins: A betting game in which the player with the lowest score on a hole wins the pot. If two or more players tie at the lowest score, the pot is carried over and added to the pot for the next hole.

Skull: To hit the ball above its center, usually on a chip or a bunker shot, causing it to travel too far.

Sky: To hit too much underneath the ball sending it much higher than intended.

Skywriting: A bad swing in which the clubhead makes a loop at the top of the backswing and comes down with disastrous results.

Slice: An uncontrollable shot that curves strongly to the right.

Slope: Gradient of the ground.

Slope Rating: A measurement of the difficulty of a course for bogey golfers relative to the **course rating**.

Slump: A period of bad play.

Smother: To hit down on the ball so that it travels a short distance on the ground.

Snake: A very long putt that travels over several breaks in the green.

Snap-Hook: To hit a hot with an acute hook.

Snipe: A ball that is hooked and drops quickly.

Sole: The bottom of the clubhead.

Sole Plate: The metal plate on the bottom of woods.

SPGA: Senior Professional Golf Association.

Spike Mark: A mark made on the green by the cleats of a golf shoe.

Spot Putting: A method of putting in which the player aims at a spot instead of directly at the hole.

Spray: To hit the ball erratically.

Spring: The flexibility of the club shaft.

Square Stance: Placing your feet in a line parallel to the direction you which the ball to travel.

Stableford: A tournament scoring method that uses points instead of strokes.

Stance: The position of a player's feet during his address.

Starter: A person who determines the order of play from the first tee.

Stick: The pin in the hole.

Stimpmeter: An instrument for measuring the speed of greens. It's a 30-inch aluminum trough raised to a 20-degree angle. A golf ball is placed on top of the trough and released to roll down on to the green. The distance it rolls after leaving the trough is then converted to a Stimp reading.

Stipulated Round: The number of holes to be played as determined by the committee during a competition.

Stony: To hit a ball close to the flagstick.

Straightaway: A hole having a straight fairway.

Straight-Faced: A club with little or no loft on the face.

Strike Off: To drive from the tee.

Stroke: A swing at the ball with the intention of hitting it.

Stroke & Distance: A penalty in which one stroke is added to the player's score, and he has to play the shot again from where he last played.

Stroke Play: A competition in which the total number of strokes for one round, or a pre-determined number of rounds, determines the winner

Stymie: When an object such as a tree lies between a player's ball and the green.

Sudden Death: When the score is tied after completing the round in a match or stroke competition, play continues until one player wins a hole.

Summer Rules: Ordinary play according the Rules of Golf.

Surlyn: Material from which most golf balls are made.

Swale: A shallow depression or dip in the ground.

Sweet Spot: The preferred spot on the clubface with which to strike the ball.

Swing: The action of striking the ball.

Swing Weight: Measurement of a club's weight.

Tap In: A very short putt.

Tee:

- A small device used to elevate the golf ball from the ground.
- The area in which the ball is place for the first shot of a hole.

Tee Off: To play a tee shot.

Tee Up: To begin play by placing a ball on the tee.

Tee Box: The rectangular area within which a player must place his ball. It is defined by the markers and two club lengths behind them.

Tee Shot: A shot played from a tee.

Teeing Ground: Same as 'Tee Box'.

Temporary Green: A green used in the winter to save the permanent green.

Texas Wedge: What the putter is called when it used from off the green. Also a shot played with a putter from outside the putting green.

Thin: A shot in which the ball is hit above center when the head of the club is following too high a line.

Thread: To play the ball through a narrow opening.

Three Ball: A game where three players compete against each other

Three-Putt: Taking three putts to hole the ball

Threesome:

- A group of three players playing together.
- A two against one match with the two partners playing alternating strokes against a single player.

Tight Fairway: A narrow fairway.

Toe: The part of the club farthest from where in joins the shaft.

Toe Job: A shot hit too close to the toe of the club.

Top: To hit the ball above its center causing it to roll or hop on the ground.

Topspin: The forward rotation of the ball.

Touch Shot: A delicate shot of great accuracy.

Tour: A series of tournaments for professionals.

Tournament: A competition in which a number of golfers compete.

Trap: A sand or grass hazard.

Trajectory: The flight path of the ball.

Triple Bogey: A score of 3 strokes over par on a hole.

Trolley: A two or three-wheeled device used to aid the carrying of a golf bag around the course.

Trouble Shot: A shot taken from a bad lie such as in a bunker or rough.

Turn: The change from front nine to back nine or vice versa.

Underclubbing: Using a club that does not yield the needed distance.

Underspin: Backspin.

Unplayable Lie: A lie from which it is impossible to play the ball such as inside a bush.

Up: A golfer's lead in strokes or holes over an opponent.

Up & Down: Taking two strokes from the current position (usually a rough or bunker) to hole the ball. In other words; one shot to bring the ball up and the next shot to play the ball down the hole.

Uphill Lie: A position of the ball on a slope in which a right-handed golfer's left foot is higher than his right foot.

Upright Swing: A swing in which the club is carried directly backward and upward from the ball.

USGA: United States Golf Association.

Vardon Grip: See 'Overlapping Grip'.

Waggle: A preliminary movement of the clubhead behind and over the ball in preparation to the swing.

Water Hazard: A hazard that contains water.

Water Hole: A hole with water such as a stream or lake that forces the players to play their balls over it.

Wedge: An iron with a heavy flange on the bottom and a high loft.

Whiff: To swing and miss the ball.

Whipping: The thread or twine wrapped around the area where the shaft joins the head. It's often replaced by a plastic ferrule.

Whippy: A very flexible shaft.

Wind Cheater: A shot played low against the wind. It is played with strong backspin, starts low and rises only toward the end of the shot.

Winter Rules: Local rules that allow a golfer to improve the lie of the ball on the fairway.

Wood: Formerly a club with a wooden head. Now the term pertains to a club that has a large head of wood, metal or other material.

Wormburner: A hard hit ball that stays close to the ground.

Wrong Ball: According to the rules, a wrong ball is any ball that is not the layer's ball in play, his provisional ball or his second ball played under the rules.

Yardage Chart: A printed card detailing the layout and yardage of each hole on the course.

Yips: A bout of nerves that make it difficult for a player to putt properly.

ABOUT THE AUTHOR

I am blessed and fortunate for being able to engage in my life's two great passions: golf and corporate training, both of which I enjoy to the fullest – and I even get paid for it. Both passions have nothing to do with one another, so I call them my 'two separate lives'.

In my 'golf life' I get to not only play this beautiful game, but I also get the opportunity to work with budding golfers who are just starting out. It gives me great satisfaction to see the joy in their faces when their game improves rapidly. Seeing them hitting longer and more accurately, and getting their whole game in shape fills me with pride. I sometimes even get beaten by some of my students on the course, which is the ultimate compliment for me as it shows that I have done a good job. Follow my golf blog here: http://www.LearnAboutGolf.com

In my 'Corporate Training life' I teach small, medium and large companies the ins and outs of digital marketing. This includes courses on Social Media Tactics, digital Advertising, e-Commerce and the likes. I am a certified Google Partner and Google Educator, and I have the great pleasure to travel extensively to share some of my expertise with my clients. To find out more connect with me on LinkedIn:
https://www.linkedin.com/in/drfrankpeter/
or search LinkedIn for 'Dr. Frank J. Peter, Ph.D.'

Printed in Great Britain
by Amazon

61912021R00158